Steam Rising Up from the Soul

For Lynn Thanksgiving
with happy
memories! Hope we
meet again!

Karen Ethelsdattar

ALSO BY KAREN ETHELSDATTAR

Earthwalking & Other Poems (Xlibris)

Thou Art a Woman & Other Poems (Xlibris)

CHAPBOOKS

Woman Artists & Woman as Art

The Cat Poems

Joan Ziz

Steam Rising Up from the Soul

Poems by

Karen Ethelsdattar

Library of Congress Control Number: 2006903785
ISBN: Hardcover   1-4257-1432-3
                         Softcover   1-4257-1431-5

This book was printed in the United States of America.

Cover painting, "Cactus Dance" ©2006 by Rena Vandewater, *renachet@aol.com*
Cover design by Erika Cushen Reesor, ReesorDesign@comcast.net

List of illustrations: Frontispiece, Drawing by Joanzia, ©2006
#2 Drawing by Joanzia, ©2006
#3 Drawing by Earl Anthony Giaquinto, ©2006
#4 Drawing by Joanzia, ©2006
#5 Drawing by Joanzia, ©2006
#6 Drawing by Joanzia, ©2006
#7 Drawing by Joanzia, ©2006
#8 Drawing by Sally B. Elliott, ©2006
#9 Drawing by Sally B. Elliott, ©2006
#10 Drawing by Sally B. Elliott, ©2006

To order additional copies of this book, contact:
Xlibris Corporation
1-888-795-4274
www.Xlibris.com
Orders@Xlibris.com
30470

The following poems have previously appeared in these publications:

Calyx, "I want to undo you"

Connors, Ginny Lowe, ed., *To Love One Another: Poems Celebrating Marriage*, "Anniversary Poem"

Community Church, New York, *Community Connections*, May 2006, "Dear Cat"

Community Church, New York, *Community News, Too!* "Eurydice, A Riddle," "Light, Part V," "Sitting here," "Waving"

Creations, "One yellow leaf"

Dream Network Journal, "Dream Landscape," "Dreamt about War"

Ethelsdattar, Karen, *Woman Artists & Woman as Art*, "Sea Travels," "Pilar Rioja dances Federico Garcia Lorca's 'Tener la Esperanza Muerte,'" "Pilar Rioja dances 'La Farruca'"

Golabek, Mona, WQXR's *The Romantic Hours*, "On Listening to Felix Mendelssohn's 'Songs without Words'"

Martz, Sandra Haldeman, *If I Had My Life to live Over I Would Pick More Daisies*, anthology, "The first time I married"

PakTribune, Internet, "Iraq, May 2004"

Phantasm, "Them Salad Days"

Twinless Times, "Never" (published as "Shakespeare's 'King Lear'")

Voices: Journal of the American Academy of Psychotherapists, "I've woven a new dream"

In Memoriam

Marion Klobucher, Teacher, Mentor, Friend

When one of Muhammad's followers ran up to him crying, "My Mother is dead; what is the best alms I can give away for the good of her soul?" the Prophet, thinking of the heat of the desert, answered instantly, "Water! Dig a well for her, and give water to the thirsty."[1]

[1]   Smith, Huston, *The World's Religions*, HarperSan Francisco, ©1991, p.249

Acknowledgements

Gratitude to my daughter, Erika Cushen Reesor and my son, Andrew Cushen for technical support & for their faith & encouragement; to my cover artist, Rena Vandewater, and artists Sally B. Elliot, Joanzia, and Earl Anthony Giaquinto for illustrations & for their faith & encouragement.

Of course, thanks be to the members of my women artists group, Women on the Edge, for their support and nurture.

And to all those friends, readers & well wishers who support and nourish me in my life and as a poet.

Contents

v

The weight of this sad time we must obey,
Speak what we feel, not what we ought to say.

Shakespeare, "King Lear"

Steam Rising Up from the Soul

Steam Rising Up from the Soul

On a rainy evening in November, in Meridian, Idaho,
I have climbed a flight of steps to enter the artist's studio.
Paintings surround me. I drink in their forms, their colors,
a Garden of Eden.
I return to look at two paintings again & again.
They are both mysterious as dreams.
One painting signals that it shall be the cover
for my third book of poems.
I see, immediately, that the title will have to change.

Let me describe it for you.
There is a large square yellow table.
Cornered across it is a checkered cloth
of red & yellow.
On the cloth is a very large cup
with a flowered border, steaming.
With one foot off the table, resting on faith, on air,
is one of Rena Vandewater's madonnas,
little, clad in a long red flowered dress,
& wearing Rena's emblem tennis shoes.
A golden halo surrounds her dark hair.
Both arms are lifted;
one arm points to the cup,
from which three rivers of steam
rise into the air.
Below the table is a very small elk,
with huge antlers, which rise to protect & embrace
the table & cup & saucer & Madonna.
A field of flowering cactuses dances below.
An oval white flowered frame
surrounds table, Madonna, elk, & antlers.

The title of my book shall be *Steam Rising Up from the Soul*.
It is a miracle how my beloved friend Rachel led me to this painter.
It is a miracle that I am taking home this painting
to hang on my wall; to wake, every day, my soul.

The doors stand open

for Black Olive

The doors stand open.
To what I am
To what I was
To what I will be.
To what I want to be
To what I never was.

I am a daughter of Spider Woman[1]
dancing in a web
of my own spinning.

I am a daughter of Changing Woman,[2]
& have moved on,
am already opening new doors,
spinning a new web.

---

[1]   Spider Woman or Spider Grandmother is a Hopi, Pueblo and Navajo God made in order that she might create life. She is a friend and has to do with weaving, protecting the People from stinging insects and teaching them things about corn planting. She has been given the power to help create life and the knowledge, wisdom and love to bless all beings she creates. (Moon, Sheila, *Changing Woman and Her Sisters*, c1984 by the Guild for Psychological Studies Publishing House).

[2]   Changing Woman is the favored figure among the Navajo Holy People. Her cosmic cyclic movements—aging each winter and becoming a beautiful young maiden each spring—make Her the essence of death and rebirth, signature of the continual restoration and rejuvenation of Life. She stands for peace and ever-renewed creation. Her gifts to people are rites and ceremonies. She is kind, gives songs, creates the horse, decrees fertility and sterility. This aspect of the Feminine is creative changing, is the capacity to flow, is cyclic time, is earth and water, is a bringing together. (Moon, Sheila, *Changing Woman and Her Sisters*)

The Daydreamer

The daydreamer, the bluestocking,
the girl with her nose in a book
when she should have been cleaning her room,
the girl who read under the bedcovers
with a flashlight, getting caught again & again,
the young wife who burnt supper
because she was trying to read a book
at the same time she cooked,
the young mother who stayed up late
& wouldn't come to bed with her husband
because she was reading,
because she was writing poems,
this girl, this woman, this mother
has now dreamed & written & published
a book of her own.

I did not know how to celebrate

With thanks to Kathy, who told me this should be a poem

The first time I published a poem
I did not know how to celebrate success
I did not know how to fling my arms wide
& thank the universe.
I did not know how to jump for joy
or multiply my gladness by sharing the news
with friend after friend.
Oh, I knew how to sorrow
& how to hesitate
& feel inadequate
& fear there wouldn't be a next poem
& a next & a next . . .
but I did not know how to celebrate,
how to celebrate & Celebrate & CELEBRATE!

"Light, Part V"

(Kei Takei's MOVING EARTH Dance Company)

You stand erect
& you fall down,
you fall over,
& you pick yourself up
& sometimes
someone helps you up
& you fall down,
you roll over,
& even if
someone helps you up
you have to help yourself
to really make it
& even so
you fall down again
& sometimes
one is the stronger
& helps the other
& sometimes
the other is stronger
& you fall down
sometimes one at a time
sometimes all together
& you pick yourself up
sometimes all together
sometimes one at a time
& you fall down
& you pick yourself up,
rising out of the inner light,
gazing upward
because the sun reminds you
of the light within
& you fall down
& you pick yourself up
& we're all in it
together.

Subway

The express train streaks past
station platforms
staccato mirages of light
thrust
      briefly
            against
the blackness of the journey
underground.
They gleam alluring
the stops not taken
transformed by speed
glittering
as a child's glimpse
of the lady circus rider
distant
in the
ring.

I'd like to give off sounds!

I'd like to give off
sounds
when I'm working!
Not necessarily fireworks,
though I kinda dig the idea of sparks,
like from the generator my father had
in his physics lab.
Something steady, maybe,
like the swish of the dishwasher,
or the perking of the coffeepot.
Not the whine of an electric saw
nor the drill digging down in the street,
but some kind of song mirror
misted with my breath
letting me know that I'm getting
something done.
I wouldn't even mind
the squeal of an inner teakettle
saying something in me has come to a boil
& is ready to pour.
I'd like to give off
sounds
when I'm working!

O rare flower

O rare flower
of the Queen of the Night plant
from Brazil to Malaysia
to Suzanne to Mako
to my friend Earl
to me.
You bloom only once in a few years,
& this is my first bloom from you
(one died before it came to full radiance).
I know it will take a week
or a week & a half till you are in full flower,
& then you will only last 8 to 12 hours.
But that you bloom at all is a miracle,
like a poem coming after many dry months.
As a yawn begets a yawn from those who witness it,
& a smile begets a smile,
so, as you begin to bloom,
I, too, begin to bloom.
As I water you,
I water my inner garden,
hoping for poem upon poem,
year upon year.
O poems be not rare.

Those precious few moments

Those precious few moments
in the morning
or after a nap
when a dream
or the first line of a poem
can slip the halter
& canter away,
not to be grasped by the mane,
but approached gently,
perhaps, with a sweet bite
of the golden apple
of consciousness,
before you stretch,
before you turn over,
before you enter the day.

"Gone Fishing"

Today we drove to Paterson, New Jersey,
William Carlos Williams' town.
In my own life
for a long time
poems have been the last thing on my mind.
We rode a ways on Paterson Plank Road,
that smooth tar surface
over the crumbling logs from an old corduroy road,
among the first of its kind.

Walking around Williams' town,
looking at the faces of ordinary people, ordinary women.
Old women with faces worn down by time.
Wondering if he delivered their babies.
Young women—
I wondered if he was there at their birthing,
Dr. Williams. Poet Williams.

We sat by the Falls on the Passaic River
that must have been there
when it was Indian country all around,
eating mozzarella & prosciutto on Italian bread.

My thoughts were that even a poet
can hang a sign on her door sometimes
that says "Gone Fishing"
& sit looking at the Falls
in William Carlos Williams' town.
Just sit there holding a pole
with an unbaited hook
& leave the poems somewhere
deep under the water
& wriggle her toes in the mud.

what creature ?

what creature is it can't speak   ?
not curse
nor sing

the
giraffe ?

I, too, am sometimes so long-throated
even a torrent of words can't force
its way up and out

I, too, bending down to drink
from the springs of my life
lower myself on wobbly legs
stage
by
uncertain stage
tremblingly vulnerable, then
to death

out of the wound

out of the wound   the child the poem
the brilliant healing scarlet flood:
bleeding is gooD
out of the rock   the rivers run
out of the wound in the earth
affirM affirM   comes all growth

out of the wound in the earth
the trees the wheat the fruit of the vine
grow green grow blond grow rich and red and dark
and wounded beyond   return
re-wounding the earth:
the Source   the Strength
      and the gentle holdingnesS

i gather earth gathers i gather Strength
to be wounded again
affirM affirM that terrible gentlenesS

Painting bamboos[1]

She
"He who learns to paint bamboos places a stalk of bamboo
in the clear moonlight so that its shadow falls on a white wall;
in this way the real shape of the bamboo comes out."

I would be the bamboo which casts a shadow on a white wall.
I would be the shadow.
I would be the white wall.
I would be the indelible pine soot ink which allows no second thoughts.
I would be the silk.
I would be the hermit of the West Lake, "Who writes in order to express
his heart."
her

---

[1] Source of quotes unknown

Seeking mastery

Seeking mastery through Zen archery
a philosopher spent years
drawing, sustaining, and letting go his breath;
grasping, raising, and drawing his bow
aimed toward that moment he should hit the mark;
so exhausting mind, effort, and willful doing
that a shot was loosed out of, at last,
that tension which yields grace:
The bow arched till it must let go the arrow
The cup filled till it must of itself spill over
The sun spewing heat careless of whether
it reaches earth to warm humankind or
dissipates.

Loving poem-ing

Loving poem-ing
is like loving New York
like loving myself
like loving anybody,
everybody . . .
a godawful unholy mixture.

Loving poem-ing is waiting
beyond patience
for a clear day with an iced-tea breeze
bringing the lost reminder
that I live in a port city,
city on the sea.

Is walking beyond bravery
along dim streets
knowing any shadow could take form
& seize me
fearing men who lurk
around unidentified corners
in doorways
with knives;
not knowing
which windows
hold random snipers.

Loving poem-ing
is like walking out into morning
(forecast: rain)
to feel the broad hand
of the sun.

Is a whiff from a hidden garden
neighboring
a noseful of garbage, of gasoline.

"Sea Travels"

for Anita Thacher

". . . fingering the stones which cannot be brought home
because their beauty is of the water & its movements & the sun . . . [1]

Twelve short films were scheduled—
yours was second;
after it, I left,
carrying "Sea Travels" like a flower
out into the rain,
like an umbrella of flowers
against the January rain . . .

A crowd of memories jostle one another,
rustling like the jonquils I arrange
each April,
then give way to the one memory
standing patiently
stilly waiting
like my first glimpse
of you, Anita,
carrying the mystery of the city,
of yourself,
of life itself
tangled in your dark gypsy hair
& your soft harsh low voice
& the rich profusion
of your dress . . .

Choose between the sea waves
waves of memory
crashing like cymbals
thundering like bass notes

---

[1]   Ethelsdattar, Karen, Woman Artists & Woman as Art, c1992

over & around
the pebbles on the beach
more pebbles, more stones
than we could imagine . . .

Choose between the movement of these waves
fluid as memory
as the wind
skirting through treetops
flirting with leaf after leaf . . .
between their movement
& something like it, rhythm
frozen in a jewel, a poem,
a still photograph, one chord . . .

Choose,
must we choose?
Aren't you, weren't you
like me, Anita,
a hungry little girl,
a woman with an appetite
for all of life . . .
so why stint memory . . .

Dive into the water, slap,
& stroke to the other side.
Hey! Arrival! & still a child!
. . . not castrati with thin high voices
& grownup bodies . . .
but women
but also children within . . .
like your dog George
splashing & woofing happily
in circles
not worried
about leaving or reaching any shore.

Like the little girl
in the red pinafore
rolling, rolling in the grass
her hands poised
to push on over again
as they glance off the ground
bony with roots
& feathered with grass,
like the hair on Father's chest.
Feel how ferris wheel dizzy,
only the hay smell, the grass smell
instead of cotton candy,
instead of a warm body . . .

Freeze the moment
or let it go
gather handfuls of pebbles
to let them fall back
through your fingers

& remember
there will be more
there will always be more.

Pilar Rioja dances Federico Garcia Lorca's "Tener la Esperanza Muerta"

September 5, 1991

Stage left sit 2 guitarists & cantaor, the flamenco singer;
three males dressed in black & white.

Center stage sits an empty chair,
draped in an arc with a long white veil whose ends stream onto the floor.

As the light rises, Rioja appears
in a fawn-colored jersey dress,
a second skin that bells at sleeve end, at dress hem.

A moving sculpture,
her body begins to explore what it is, what it can do,
bending & slow-stretching, arcing at the waist,
hand grazing a thigh; hands raised, suppliant.

The veil waits on the empty chair,
white as moonlight,
for the moment she will approach it,
lift it into existence.
We are one, the audience. We withhold our breath.

How she moves to the chair, inevitably,
& claims the veil, I forget,
but the stage fills with illusion
as her body dreams wedding dreams,
her body exists only to unite
with a man's, a bridegroom's.

Ominously, the canes of the musicians strike the floor,
a stark sound
waking the dreamer in her, in us, harshly,
sounding & resounding doom, faster.

Dancer tangles in white bridal veil,
helpless insect in spider's web,
choking in the snowy folds of her dreams,
thrashing,
tragic.

What happens,
what happens?
That once proud head
emerges with sudden thrust
from cluster of white veil,
from fisherman's net,

confronts unthinkable life,
not to be betrothed,
not to marry,
not to mother.

Her visage, stunned, bewildered,
widowed,
cries, "Where am I?"
The lights go down
& we look, not at the dancer
but into our own darkness.

Pilar Rioja dances La Farruca

(An answer to Lorca's "Tener la Esperenza Muerta")

The woman gowned elaborately
in teal blue with sequins,
in scarlet & black, with ornate hair comb,
with tiers of ruffles,
with fringed shawls,
made her way in a man's world
by fierceness & flirtation
with a kind of arrogance.
Vigilant to defend her own beauty,
poised like a snake to strike.

Again we meet the face of the woman
without hope of marriage,
rising now out of the throat of a white broadcloth man's shirt,
renewed & vulnerable;
the sweet curves of her woman's body
contained in lampblack high-waisted trousers
& the firm fabric of a man's short black vest.
She has become the torero,
the man who never arrived to embrace her.
Her femininity is braided around her own spine.
She is more than bride, wife, or mother.
Resolute, fluid, she embodies the best of both woman & man.

La Farruca halts
as the dancer's feet find one another,
stand close together, side by side.
Her body swoops low,
one arm extended,
as though to display crimson cape to the bull,
but he, with the audience, is already vanquished,
& she, the woman, the artist, the dancer, victorious.
Olé!

Brooding Great Mother

(on an untitled sculpture by Ole Langerhorst)

Two small beings
emerge from an egg
contained & brooded over
by a large-eyed one
with beak & wing & claw.
O great hovering mother,
the cave of your being,
back in the beginning,
back before the beginning,
was harbor so safe
there was not even a word
for safeguard, safekeeping.

Portrait of a wall

(From a photograph by Sudhir Vaikkattil)

This pocked plaster wall
with a single poster tacked to it
& pinholes from other tacks
next to mysterious stains.
Books, journals, papers piled against it
by someone whose mind is on fire,
who knows just where to find
the book with this passage,
the paper with that.
A reader's room,
A writer's room,
A thinker's room,
A room whose beauty is usefulness.
A room which people with minds will visit.
A room to cradle the candle of the intellect.
A room where hands reaching for books
will find them.

Room with lightbulb

Poem on a photograph by Sudhir Vaikkattil

A lightbulb with no shade
will suffice to read, to select
one record from the stack,
to live a life that is minimal,
& graceless.
One bare lightbulb belongs
in a nudist colony
where people meet determinedly
without mystery
& one longs for theatre
or for a nineteenth century lady
half-concealing her face
with an unfurled fan.
This naked bulb
is like a stripped winter tree
that has forgotten
what it is like to be leaved
that has forgotten
other seasons.

This towel

(on a photograph by Sudhir Vaikkattil)

Nothing was ever new
in this bathroom
but this towel
& fresh rolls of toilet paper.
This towel has come
overdressed to the party
This towel married beneath itself
& tries to ignore
the peeling paint on the steam pipe.
Mutters that it deserved a better fate
than to be hung on a nail,
brushing against the cracked & patched & whitewashed
bathroom wall,
looking down on a dwindling roll
of toilet paper.
This towel pretends in its dreams
& its finer moments
that it is a velvet cloak
entering a ballroom.
This towel dreams of an exquisite owner
with skin of silk
wrapped in its folds
& about to enter a passionate love affair.
This towel does not know what it is
to be threadbare & ragged.
This towel supposes it will be velvet & proud forever.
Like a well-watered summer lawn
it does not believe in drought
or winter.

This chair

(from a photograph by Sudhir Vaikkattil)

I could make up a story
about this chair
in this corner,
its back against the radiator coils
under a larder of filled bookshelves.
One glance at the titles:
Silences by Tillie Olsen,
a biography of John Keats
& another of D.H. Lawrence
& I already love the owner.
I want to sit myself in this armchair
with the folded blanket padding the back,
& another blanket piled on the seat,
ready to wrap my legs on a winter night
till the early morning light comes in through the window
to nourish the plant on the sill
& the reader in the chair.
I could live in this chair.
I could die in this chair,
& even death would come cozily.

These clothes

(on a photograph by Sudhir Vaikkattil)

These clothes
on thin wire hangers from the drycleaners
hooked over the rope knotted to a pipe.
There aren't many of them;
they must belong to someone
who's moving in
or moving out
or living poorly.
The sleeve of the plaid shirt
shyly touches the arm of the vertical pipe,
not quite daring to embrace it.
The other arm doesn't quite rub shoulders
with the pants—they hang
properly, a just sufficient distance apart.
The back of the shirt
buttoned carefully
with its sleeves hanging awkward & empty
hides the top of the dress
& the folded trousers hide the body
of the shirt.
In front of the shirt are several empty hangers.
They could be riders in a subway train
crammed close together
but avoiding taking notice of each other.
These are not clothes,
these are not hangers
who have managed to afford a closet.

Survivor

(on a photograph by Sudhir Vaikkattil)

Towel with fringe of ragged edges
& damp & scent of soap
Soft with use
& worn as an old elephant's hide
as a child's stuffed animal
Dark & threadbare towel
slung on a dimestore towel rack
hung on the plaster of a white wall
cracked & bulging with clumsy patches.
Hung over the stained white enamel tub
of a thousand tenements.
Tired towel.
Towel that winces as it's thrown
in the laundry basket,
raw skin pulling back from the washing machine.
Shredded towel that no longer even dreams
of the days when it was velvet & proud & splendid.
Survivor.
Dear ragged survivor.

Epiphanies

I like to watch the competence of hands:
a professional shoeshine man
with his cloths, brushes, waxes, liquids,
ointments;
his hands that work with a flourish
building the shine
like an artist building up layers of paint
on a canvas.

He cleans, applies color
(using a narrow brush just to paint
the edges of the soles),
& he buffs & he polishes,
snapping his stained cloth in the air.

Once or twice
my mother or father
bought me a shine.
I don't remember ever buying one
for my daughter or son.
I want to ask if they've ever had a shoeshine.
I want to buy them a shine,
watch them climb into the seat,
rest their feet on the metal feet
& yield themselves
to that ancient rite of coming of age.

I like to watch the competence of hands:
the driver of an old bus
without power steering,
both hands spanning the wheel
as he maneuvers the body of the bus

around a rough corner—
the strength of his arms behind his hands
& his shoulders behind his arms.
Then his right hand clenched around the knob of the gear shift,
relinquishing it only to send the coin machine
into its clackety rhythm, counting, counting . . .

I like to watch the competence of hands.

The jacket & the chair & the hat

Yogui is painting a cabinet in the kitchen.
I am sitting in a chair at the table
watching him. We are talking.

Opposite me is his green outer jacket
spread over the back of another chair,
topped by his brown suede hat,
with a Mexican woven sash wound round about it,
just over the brim.

It is like I am looking into the face of a shaman,
a faceless face which nevertheless sees & hears
& understands.

It is a poem. It is a painting.
Suddenly I remember where I have seen something like it,
Magritte's painting *The Healer*,
cape spread over the back of the chair,
which held a bird cage,
topped by a hat.

How did this painting happen?
Did Magritte one day without thinking
hang his cape on the back of a chair,
placing his hat on top?
Was there a bird cage already sitting on that chair?

& did he feel there the presence of some sort of healer,
psychiatrist or shaman, inhabiting the room with him?
The two souls sitting, a bird in the depths of the cage,
& one perched outside the open cage door.
& did he truly paint what was already there,
where inner reality & outer come together?

The Magician (*Poem Anita said*)

He does all the traditional things
like sawing a woman in thirds.
He shows the feet waggling at one end
& the head is talking throughout at the other end
& nothing in between.
Not even any blood.

You see her lie down.
Then they come with a box & put it over her.
Then they come with the swords.

They take the middle section out.
They pass their hands through the empty middle.
They take the middle box away.

Where does the woman go?
Whose legs are they?

Poems People Said

Poem Andrew said

Airplane at night

Hey! Look at that star
running away!

Poem Kevin said
on losing his first tooth

Now I have a skylight
in my mouth

2nd poem Earl said

In some corner of my mind
there's always a silkworm
eating mulberry leaves
to spin silk
for my wedding gown.

Poem Earl said

I consider all relationships
to be mirrors
& you have to know
which smudges are yours,
& which are the other person's.

Poem Sophie said

I'm kind of prowling
around a question
I don't know what
to do with.

Poem Jessica said

I've spent my whole life
in this Jackson Pollack mode—
my life, my house,
my relationships.

2nd Poem Jessica said

I'm an only child,
& the sun rose & set
in my belly button.

Poem Yogui said

We play tricks on ourselves
because of the things we believe,
we don't believe,
& the things we want to believe.

2nd Poem Sophie said

I'm becoming more & more
friendly with my sloppiness:
it's a treat I can allow myself,
like chocolate.

3rd Poem Sophie Said

It was mostly anxiety
though it dressed itself
in fancy colours.

Poem Joan said

I wish I had a fairy god-spouse
to come & help me
clean up the house!"

Poem Joan said when I yawned on the telephone

A musical yawn,
kind of like Baudelaire writing
about his cat meowing.

Poem Kathy Stone said

I just kind of put my whole life
on hold
& worried for a week.

Poem anonymous friend said

I must go now.
I have company coming
& I've got to vacuum up
the toenails & tangerine seeds
from my carpet.

Poem Kathy Frey said

Taking a biscotti in one hand
& a ripe red cherry in the other,
Kathy said, laughing,
"So I won't be lonely."

Poem Jerry said

I always bare my soul
to the man in the token booth.

2nd poem Jerry said

It seems like
I'm always a victim
of anticipation
or regret.

3rd poem Jerry said

When I can find myself
I confound myself.

Poem Bruce said

I really struggle a lot
with my body & my weight
& my mind
& its weight.

Memories Of Madness:
The 1 On The Telephone Dial

ONE

I clung to the 1 and was cloven
by the blade of this knife.
Divided, myselves clung still
and were reunited.

I clung to the 1:
As it spun
I hung.

I clung to the 1 as it
swung on its axis,
plunged through the circle,
I plunged.

I clung to the 1:
like a chant
I sung,
lest I be undone
One One One.

As I laid my head on my husband's breast,
darkness roared down in an avalanche,
laying the vision of line and circle to rest.
The beat of his heart swelled into the
beat of the universe.
We were one with its thunder.
We were drowned in its thunder.
There was only the thunder.

ONE ONE ONE

A phone is a phone is a telephone

The year moves into October.
The year moves toward October nineteen,
the anniversary of the birth of a son,
& with him in my arms it moves on to October 31,
All Saints' Eve, Hallowe'en,
the eve of the anniversary of the death of my sister, my twin.

The telephone rings. It rings in memory. It rang then.

"Nancy died within the hour."
the hour
our Nancy
Nancy
Oh, Nancy
No.

The telephone.

Ted's dead.
Ted's dead. In Berkeley. Dead. From cirrhosis of the liver at thirty.
Left his new wife & fresh start & baby son. Left.
His sweet clarinet laid aside
& his other woman, that raunchy blues guitar
he'll make love to no more.
Left those giant thumbprints in the underside of his pot.
Left the recollection of midnight in a foundry by the railroad tracks,
a train screeching through the dark outside
white hot molten metal in a crucible within
& Ted like some sorcerer's assistant in the eerie light.
Ted stumbling larger than life into the library
carrying the battered green music box retrieved from the attic
from what was left of what was ever home
& it sounding tinnily, loud in the silence,
Ted muttering, "Gotta give it away to Mike's kid,
can't keep it, it tears me up."

The telephone.

Dear crazy Randy, dear randy Randy blew her brains out
blew them out with a shotgun in an Ohio barn.
Strange violent death for a woman. Christ, Strange violent
death for a man, for anyone.
Victim of her own cruel jokes to the bitter end,
coarse & crude & underneath it all so fuckin' tender.
Randy, you were so gutsy, so fuckin' tough
& there must've been a better way to let it all hang out.

The telephone.

The telephone is the instrument of death.
No. the telephone is only a telephone.
Karen, pick up the telephone.

Speak. Listen.
The telephone is a telephone
& sometimes brings life.
Speak. Listen.
I want to live. I want to live. I want to live.
Anna Karenina. The railroad tracks. Pull yourself back.
Anna, wife of Karenin. Karen. The railroad tracks.
A crucible of molten metal in the night.
I want life.
Camille. Ophelia. Face in the water.
Lazarus. Christ.
Mary, Virgin or Magdalen. One or the other. The twins. Which one?
I didn't die. I didn't die. I didn't die.
The left & the right
Left or right
Left Left I am left.

The sharps closet.
We'll protect you against yourself.
Because they take the scissors away I know fear.
Scissors, razors, you could do yourself in on most anything.
If, then. Everything.
Everything's an instrument of terror.
The devil's invention, the sharps closet.
The devil's invention, the closet, closet anything.
Because they locked them away I know fear.

Because they locked me away.
Because, because.
You could do yourself in.
You could do yourself in on most anything.

I let a cup of water drop from my hand.
My friend sees with horror.
She does not understand.
Death by water. Death by fire. Death by earth. Death by air.
And let this cup pass.
Death by the telephone.

Karen, forget.
The doctor knows best.
He tests me.
"Count to 100."

I count perfectly, forward & backward.
I count perfectly, backward.

"What does this mean?
'People who live in glass houses
shouldn't throw stones'?"
I sob, "People who are very fragile
themselves shouldn't hurt
other people."

Next question.
"A rolling stone gathers no moss."
"A rolling stone. A rolling stone.
Moss. Don't know. Can't answer"

I am the doctor.
I want to remember.
Where I have gone I swear to remember.
Everything. I will not have taken this journey
for nothing.
I write. I tear it up.
The nurse goes for the wastebasket.
"What did you write?" "Nothing."
Karen, the telephone. Speak!

"Because I do not hope to turn again
Because I do not hope
Because I do not hope to turn . . .

Because I cannot drink
There, where trees flower, and springs flow, for there is nothing again"

". . . strength beyond hope & despair
climbing the third stair."[1]

Thomas. Tom Eliot. Doubter. Believer. Brother.

"Teach us to care and not to care.
Teach us to sit still."[2]

Teach us to sit still.
Teach us to sit still.
I scream to my son from across the room
"Be still!"
He falls to the floor.
My God. What have I done.
Still. Dead. Still.
I want him to live. I want to live.
He picks himself up. He breathes.

I vow to remember everything.
I will return from hell with the living water.
I will put everything back together.

Karen, answer the telephone.
Get a job. Pick up the receiver.
"Hello, may I help you?"
"Hello, may I help you"
"Hello, may I help you?"
I couldn't help her.
I couldn't do it for her.
"Hello, may I help you?"

---

[1]   Eliot, T.S., *The Complete Poems and Plays*, Harcourt, Brace & Company ©1952, "Ash Wednesday"

[2]   Ibid.

"Sister, mother
And spirit of the river, spirit of the sea,
Suffer me not to be separated
And let me cry come unto Thee."[3]

The words, the telephone.

Odin, the hangman,
gave one eye to Mimir
to drink of the well of wisdom
at the root of the world tree.
An eye for an eye. An eye for memory.
One-eyed Odin, of the magic runes
that write the universe.
All-Father. Norseman. Hangman.
"I give you to Odin."
I give myself to Odin.

Let it be done. Let her swing.
No, let it be undone.

Done. Undone.
The words, the telephone, Karen.
The power.
Who holds the power?
Who molds the words?
Who speaks & listens into the telephone?
Karen.
Cairn, the heap of memory's stones.
Charon, the ferryman who makes it back
across the River Styx.
Styx & stones & memory's bones.
Dry bones.

Hello. Good-bye. Hello.
Karen, just plain Karen.

---

[3]   Ibid.

With hope

I do not know the color
of the flower of hope
only its odor
crushed carelessly underfoot
only its odor
bruised out of an iron fist
& carried sometimes,
only sometimes
on the wind.

Hope is the ghost
of an Indian ancestor
who loved this land
making her way up
frail & tough
through a jagged crack in the layers of pavement
taking her chance
like a blade of grass.

Hope is a cloudburst
opening with vehemence
& so soon spent
leaving the air
still charged & heavy.

Hope is the face of a trusting child
with nowhere to turn for comfort
but to the parent
who struck her.
Hope is her small cool hand
creeping into yours
scarcely daring to ask for warmth
to ask, just ask.

Hope is a night without sleep
When day breaks
it is spent.

To live without hope is death.
To live with hope, with hope
is harsh.

Crazy, crazy, crazy

Crazy, crazy, crazy
hope
with more lives
than a street cat

Crazy, crazy, crazy
hope
clumsy clown
with the smile that turns
cartwheels

Crazy, crazy, crazy
hope
trying a swan dive
& making a
belly flop

Crazy, crazy, crazy
hope
ya rose with thorns
ya unicorn

Crazy, crazy, crazy
hope:
Girl,
ya sure got
an Attitude.

It seems the journey will never end

I am a child.
I am afraid.
The exotic lady in the movie
opens a small jeweled box,
placing it on the bed.
A deadly spider crawls out of it,
crawls toward the person on that bed,
so slowly
it seems the journey will never end.

I am a child.
I am afraid.
I scream.
Daddy turns on the light.
He comes to comfort me.
He holds me.
He takes my hand.

The dream returns.
Once, Daddy held me.
Now he tells me sternly,
"You must not be afraid."

I hear him.
I grow wise as a woman.
I am learning to translate men.
I read: "You must pretend."

The dream returns,
but he will not return to hold me,
he will not return again.
I will become like men.

I will not feel. I will not need. I must pretend.

I've woven a new dream

I'll not return again for comfort
to the very father who thrashes me
with his razor strop
with his hellfire & brimstone tongue.

I dreamed one night that I screamed at him:
"You won't quit, will you
till you've splattered my ego all over the floor
& then you just stand there
Trampling it
Trampling it
Trampling it."

Out of the dark of years of nights
I've woven a new dream
I create a new father
I am bringing him into the light
I speak to him & feed him words
in a voice that is no longer a thin scream
but rich with controlled power.
His voice trembles, his hands shake
but he is learning to say:
"This is my beloved daughter
In whom I am well pleased
In whom I delight."

This dream is my talisman
This dream is my power stone
This dream is good medicine.

Hurricane Karen

There she goes again,
Hurricane Karen,
Little girl doing the dizzy dance,
the dizzy dizzy dizzy dance dance dance.
Little girl too big for her britches.
Little girl who wanted her father for a lover,
wanted him all for her own.
Who tussled in his bed Sunday mornings,
fighting sister for his Masonic ring
Who sometimes, getting it
thought she had him
but never more than a blissful moment
& she wanted him forever.
What an angry little girl
What an angry, angry little girl!
She wanted to overpower him,
scare him to death;
She wanted not to overpower him
because that scared her.
Dizzy dizzy dizzy dance
Oh how delicious to scare Daddy:
the way to his heart is through his fear
Dizzy dizzy dizzy dance
But if he gets scared so does she.
Nobody ever told that little kid
that little Svenska flicka
it's all right to want
even what you can't have.
It's all right to love so deeply
you want someone all for your very own.
And sometimes, but only sometimes
You don't have to share.

Father who taught me

Father who taught me to play with words,
along with the terror of crossing streets
even holding the largeness of your hand;
unwittingly you gave me the power
to skip narrow rope bridges
over tumbling currents,
to cross oceans in birch bark canoes,
to tread, warily, across glaciers
& to climb like a goat on mountain tops.

Father who taught me such fear of fire
that till ten years of age
I dared not strike a match myself:
you gave me words to burn,
to paint the giant conflagrations of my soul.
Unaware, you fed in me the fires of old volcanoes.

Father who taught me fear of deep water:
I swim like a fish in my dreams, in my poems.
When boat after boat capsizes under me,
words float like oars to the surface;
I hold to them & make it safely
to the shore.

Father who taught me fear of myself
& then left me at home:
You gave me myths & fairy tales,
books about journeys over land & sea
& when you came home you sang me songs,
you sang me hymns,
you read me poems.

You gave me Seven League Boots.
You gave me charms against the Snow Queen.

Penelope & Ulysses Revisited

"Peter, Peter, pumpkin eater
Had a wife & couldn't keep her
He put her in a pumpkin shell
& there he kept her very well."

—Nursery rhyme

"So I would have had him leave,
So I would have had her stand
and grieve."
　　　　　　　　—T.S. Eliot

Ulysses:　　　　I'm going off to the wars,
　　　　　　　　shipping out to sea
　　　　　　　　& you my dear
　　　　　　　　are the part of myself
　　　　　　　　which tends the hearth,
　　　　　　　　which longs for security.
　　　　　　　　Stay at your loom
　　　　　　　　& weave pretty things;
　　　　　　　　braid & unbraid & weave the sunlight in your hair,
　　　　　　　　while I adventure.
　　　　　　　　Be there, be thou there for me,
　　　　　　　　my pretty.

*　　*　　*

Ulysses returns to find Penelope gone:

Ulysses:　　　　Show me the man
　　　　　　　　who seized *my* woman
　　　　　　　　& destroyed *my* home:
　　　　　　　　I'll murder him,
　　　　　　　　& count that less than recompense.

Servant:　　　　But, Sire, she said
　　　　　　　　she was her *own* woman.
　　　　　　　　There was no other man

unless, she said,
you'd count the man within
her breast, the only man,
she said, who'd ever known
to cherish her for clothing him
with the freely woven garment of her love.

Tis true, she *was* accompanied
by another woman.
Companions-at-arms they looked,
with their hair sheared
& the light of adventure in their eyes.
I cannot tell if they were lovers . . .
when men are cloistered
or lost at sea
or off at war
or held in prison
& hear the sirens' call
& ache for a woman & there is none,
sometimes 'tis said,
they turn to other men . . .
perhaps, too, women turn to women.

"Friend" was all she called
that other woman
as they strode along
arm in arm . . .
but I've only seen such trust before
in a bride's eyes
& I've rarely seen it the morning after,
as her husband left her
fed for adventure,
clasping the key to her chastity belt,
promising to return
with all the treasures of the Orient
when all she ever wanted
was the love in his heart,
freely given.
The love *bond*, it seems,
was made for women,
& 'tis the men who seem to flee it.

But Penelope,
perhaps she was an unnatural woman,
though that was not what she named herself.
She said, "I am an honest woman."
She said, "I love, Therefore I am."

Eurydice: a riddle

Orphée's gone mad with looking for her
What, that he looked behind is why he lost her?

One only looks for what he needs to find:
"Eurydice," the name's as liquid as his tongue . . .

Ah, that he'd have the folly to seize, possess her
Whose form and rhythm dance in every StOnE.

Samson & Delilah

Samson struts in to Delilah
locks unkempt
clothing & skin
soiled with the stains
of toil & battle.
Forgiving these
she tenderly breathes,
"You're beautiful."
He smiles, taking the admiration
of women
of this woman, too,
as his due,
his eye calculating
the worth of her beauty
as his ornament.
He snatches a pomegranate
from a richly carved tray,
tumbling & bruising
a pyramid of other fruits,
kicks off his dusty sandals,
sends them flying
against a vase of desert flowers,
& rips open her silken robes.
He calls her whore
as he boasts of the women
who have beckoned him from tents unnumbered
as the sands of the desert
& of how he bedded them every one.
Samson, before your locks were ever shorn
Indeed you brought the Temple down.

I wanna tell you

"It's like the whole apartment has been raped. I threw out everything in the bedroom. It's a whole new room. I couldn't stand looking at it."

Chelsea News, June 14, 1973
account of a woman who was
raped in her apartment

I wanna tell you
every woman that's been raped
any / where any / how
was raped in her own home

& I wanna ask you
how do you paint
how disinfect
how throw out
the furnishings of your soul?

The first time I married

The first time I married
I took my husband's name for mine
& added Mrs.
I pulled it over my ears,
a woollen cap,
even when it scratched in warm weather.
I was his falcon, hooded.
I was his pigeon, banded.
I sank into his name like a feather bed
& neglected to rise in the morning.
I crept under his wing
like a fledgling
too small to spread its own feathers.

Now I add your name to mine,
proud & frightened.
This time I keep my own,
I surrender nothing.
Still this act
reminds me of captivity—
sweet & dangerous.
Forgive me when I grow fierce
& understand
when I seek wild mountain meadows.

Second Wife

I married a man whose wife had left him.
At first I only knew why she had loved him.
How could she have left him?
I hated her with his own hatred, magnified.
I hated the Deserter & what she had done to him.
I hated her for making him suffer.
I hated her for making it harder for him to trust me.

Now, because I am a woman,
Now, because I am that man's wife,
I begin to understand her better.
How shall I endure?

The Stepmother

I feel like an outsider in this home.
I feel like I've been left out in the cold.
I feel like I'm still in my mother's home
& I'm not yet grown,
& I have no home of my own.

They call me Stepmother
but I feel like the stepchild.
I feel like I don't belong.
Everyone here has belonged here
& belonged to each other
for a very long time.
Only I haven't been here before.
Only I don't belong.

I must confess

I must confess
to being a little in love
with every man
who loves a woman.
I loved them both,
young husband & wife,
for loving each other.
When she came to my house,
she greeted me with a smile,
& coming very close,
remarked how my plant was thriving:
"It's all over the place," she said.
Her voice was not smiling.
I am a divorced woman.

What's in a Name?

As though she had no mother,
She bears her father's name.
What she is called as a maiden
denies her own kind
& half her origin.

"I am Daddy's little girl;
my heart belongs to Father."

As though she were not a person
She takes her husband's name.

"I am transferred like stocks & bonds:
a solid investment
because I will never be my own."

As though she were no mother,
Her child denies her name.
Son or Daughter
Its name echoes its father.

"It is as though I
& my mother
& my mother's mother
have never been."

Them Salad Days

For Charles Perroncel, Ph.D., who helped me rescue them

This is a poem about them salad days
them green green salad days
about kisses cool as freshly rinsed lettuce
about deep parsley kisses
vine-ripened tomato & sharp scallion kisses
kisses firm & fleshy as mushrooms lifted from the earth
garlicky kisses
& kisses sprinkled with thyme
peppery kisses
& kisses with a nip of dill . . .

& about the wines sipped with those salads
sweet heavy Mogen David & port & vermouth
seafoam champagne
Liebfraumilch & fruity Pouilly Fuisse
Moselle, & the bottle of haute sauterne
that slipped from under my arm—or was it yours—
shattered, & splashed all over the floor
of a Penn Station bookstore . . .
plum wine & rice wine
& hot mulled wine in Jon's Scandinavian Shop . . .

& about the roses:
yolk golden & spun-sugar pink
eggshell & old-satin
scarlet & crimson
buds & blossoms & whole bunches
&
one
rose
of a kind
so red, so red.

about a hand caressing
a wine glass across a checkered tablecloth
& another caressing mine . . .

This is a poem fluttering out of volumes of Donne & Keats & Yeats
& Shelley & even Eliot
& always e.e. cummings . . .
a magnolia petal . . .
a gingko leaf . . .
A poem that breathes youth & age & death & birth
& remembers gladness.

"My mother said I never should play with the gypsies in the wood"

Dear Tim,

We horsed around like a couple of kids. Were kids.
Had fun even fighting.
You dashed across the country to see me.
I was thrilled. Daddy always left me. You came to me.
That was true love.
I sent you telegrams that threw the operator, who was no English major.
e e cummings et cetera.
We made it in the Glen, on the golf course, in the theatre
your dorm & your Granny's apartment.
It was scary & fun as a rollercoaster.
Alone together was beautiful.
But in public you were cynical, you put me down.
Only that made it easy to leave you,
one man I was never too much for,
who egged me on, abetted me, loved me outrageous.

Why did I bury her, that gypsy kid?
Where did I bury her for so long?

i am thinking a love poem to you

i am thinking a love poem to you.
i am thinking about how our moistures mingle.
about how the long strands of my hair
catch like tinsel on the needles of your mustache.
about the maleness & female in me
making love to the female & maleness in you.
about the softness & hard of you
making love to the hardness & soft of me.
i am thinking i am a christmas tree
& your love illumines me,
who am already green & beautiful.
i am thinking you are a christmas tree.
i am thinking a love poem to you.

Small sounds

Like the small sounds that make silence intimate:
murmur of water, trill of bird, rustle of trees.
Or like brushmarks that still and hold the eye,
faint imprint in an endless roll of landscape:
let the rare scent and touch of a drowsing child

or a lover

speak.

Sometimes

Sometimes you are so familiar to me
you seem a stranger
like myself when I come home to look in the mirror
after my hair's cut,
like a poem I wrote ten years back.

Sometimes you are so strange to me
you seem familiar,
like when you wake in the morning
muttering & gesturing like the madmen
I walk swiftly past in the streets,
or when I wake
& see you asleep.

Sometimes when you leave me I feel empty
& sometimes complete.
Sometimes I hunger for you
& hate it when you withdraw from me into sleep.
I lie listening to your breathing & your heartbeat
& cannot bear to be separate,
& sometimes I hunger to lie in my own bed,
to do things my own way,
to be apart.

Anniversary poem

Wednesday evening
we were sitting at the supper table
after sharing another meal,
feeling lazy
& kind of like playing,
batting around words & images
like a couple of kittens,
& it came to us
that next day was our Anniversary,
1 year & 1 month & 1 week & 1 day,
not Paper nor Wood nor Silver nor Golden nor Diamond
& sure enough,
Thursday
we didn't bring each other flowers,
but I had thoughts about
how when we were out walking
we smelled a sweet smell in the air
& crossed the street after it
to stand under the linden trees
& you pulled off a little blossom
& we looked at it together,
& I thought about
you on your knees with your camera
trying to capture a flurry of white butterflies
over a cluster of lavender
& I thought how I have married
the kind of man who kneels to the butterflies & the flowers,
& how I love being together on this earth,
& my thoughts were gifts.

On listening to Felix Mendelssohn's
Songs Without Words

Ah, Felix,
whose name means happiness,
whose name means bliss,
A century & a half before me
you lived my life.
A century & a half after you
I repeat your hopes, your fears
your ecstasies, & your quiet despairs.
Laying my head to rest on your breast,
giving myself up to the harbor of your arms;
such irony
that even there the storms rise in my heart,
the tears steal down my cheeks,
& the world in all its contradictions
will not leave me.
I come to you for tenderness
& yes, it is there,
but not without severity.
I come to you to forget my pain
yet even, yet especially,
in your arms it stirs again.

I travel with you
into the girlhood of my mother,
that little child with the brown eyes
who had always to wear a brown dress
& yearned for a blue dress
like her blue-eyed sister Violet's;
who in a good year got an orange
in her Christmas stocking;
who learned to read from newspapers
pasted against the drafts
coming in through the chinks
of a log cabin.
How I ache to tell that child

with the warm hazel eyes
& the dark hair now streaked with silver,
"Mother, love that little girl with the brown eyes—I do,"
if she were not hiding out of reach somewhere,
in a dark forest.

Felix, you remind me of a long ago lover,
Peter, Piero, Kamala to my Siddhartha,
the warm wind, the Sirocco,
of his passion for Masaccio,
for the Renaissance
& for his Lady, the White Goddess.

Felix, the pianoforte breathes you
& breathes out the soul of my dead sister.
She is little again
& I see her eyes, so large, so deep,
& the wistful smile still trembling on her lips.
She is skipping rope, playing hide-and-go-seek,
kick-the-can, & what was that game
with the line "Heavy, heavy hangs over thy head"?
Like Anne Boleyn, she went under the axe so young, so young—
those the gods love die early.
Oh Nancy, Nancy, No my God, let it not be Nancy,
let it not be, let it not be.
In autumn the leaves fall,
but Nancy, Nancy Lee,
she never reached autumn.

Felix, you remind me of fourteen years
of married love, of married tears.
Of night after night when
no matter what exhaustion the day brought
I knew that dark would bring
the oblivion of a husband's arms . . .
or if he turned his back on me
& shut his ears,
stalking around for days nursing grudges,
refusing to make up,
murdering me with his silence,
even that, even that.

Songs Without Words you wrote
& even they, even they,
Felix,
are passing cruel.
They cover me with tender kisses
like the star-studded blanket of the night sky,
& every kiss leaves a bruise,
Felix,
Felix Mendelssohn,
whose name means happiness.
whose name means bliss.

Sensuous moments

I. At a little Arab cigarette & jewelry shop on 6th Avenue
    in Greenwich Village, years ago,
    I was trying on a pair of silver earrings,
    having trouble inserting the wire in my pierced ear.
    The proprietor said, "Let me help you."
    Gently he took my left ear lobe between his fingers,
    & with such ease inserted the earring in question.
    To my surprise, from that gesture of a moment,
    I felt a twinge of desire.
    It lingers yet.

II. My job was counseling international students
    for college admission.
    One cold winter day an applicant from the Philippines
    came to my desk, shaking my hand & taking a chair
    beside me.
    His hand was so cold I shivered.
    His school record was mediocre,
    but something about his sweetness led me
    to spend more time with him.
    As he rose to go, he again took my hand,
    but, to my amazement, his hand was intensely warm.
    I remember this.

III. Decades ago, I was having,
    instead of walking pneumonia,
    a walking emotional breakdown.
    As my then husband & I entered the door of the laundromat
    down the street from our apartment,
    a tall, good-looking Asian man rushed past us,
    giving me for a split second such an intense look
    that I was shaken.
    My husband, noting this, asked,
    "Who was that man?"
    Truthfully I said, "I have no idea,"
    thinking to myself, "That was a god,
    perhaps Shiva."
    I have not forgotten.

Day & Night

(small poems in celebration of what never was & always will be)

The hand of Day
gathers up the strands of Night;
begins its weaving.

The hand of Night
smoothes out the furrows.
from the brow of Day.

Come, Evening
cries the Day
Diving in dying splendour
into the deepening violet
of her throat

Night calls: let's play
You be Night & I'll be Day
You be the Man in the Moon,
arms outstretched to clasp the
    Sunflower.

Between dusk & dawn
dawn & dusk
who dares, who can bear to remember
the space where each is both.

Look, the Day
rising with a smile
from the loosening arms of Night.

Hold me! cries the waning Day
Come to me! calls the Night.

The Moon
who could not wait
slips into the Mid-Day sky.

There is a land, too,
where the Sun shines
at midnight.

With tender fingers of light
Day brushes back the hair
from the eyes of Night.

Cover Midnight
with a curtain of stars
as she reels
toward the Sunrise.
drunken with desire

Look!
The Sky Woman of the Night
The Temple Courtesan
her breasts & her pubis
spangled with sequins
glittering through the veils
of the drifting clouds

Day covers his burning face
with tears of rain.

Decipher in the flickering
calligraphy of the night sky
The runes
The hieroglyphs
The Morse code
The million pin pricks of the
Braille in which Night writes
her longing for the Day.

The Sun rises
out of the last echoes of the beat of Night.
From the pause of Mid-Day
his face turns yearning
toward the gently drumming fingers of
approaching dusk.

I want to undo you

I remember the color of your shirt
aquamarine
over the brown, brown of your skin
but I never numbered its buttons.
I want to be their undoing,
I want to open those buttons
one by one.

I want to open your shirt at your throat
over your solid heart
& down, down, to your belt,
with each unfastening
the halt in an elevator
from floor to unnumbered floor,
feeling the motion between
a surge
in my womb.

I want to undo you slowly, drawing it out;
I want every inch of unfastening to last an Egyptian dynasty.

No, no
let it be quick:
swift
as scissor
through silk,
quick
like a kid
ripping tissue
from Christmas.

I want it to last . . .
let it be quick . . .
I want . . . I want . . . I want
to undo you
as I am undone.

You want to be unexpected

You want to be unexpected
as rain
in the desert.

In another life,
a cactus,
I made do with little,
& held on to what I had.

Now I am a rain dancer.
You fear
I will shake you down.
Now I am a shaman.
You fear I'll fly up
& seed the clouds.

You watch me
out of the corner of your eye
holding the brimming bowl of the sky
carefully,
with both hands,
trembling.

Dream I am the wind:
Spill
& shudder.

Tug-of-war

I tug my thoughts
        away from you
carefully
        as a kite caught
        in a tree

All the while
my heart is straining
my body eager
        to be that kite
        in the arms
        of that tree

& the Spring wind murmurs,
        no help from me,
        no help from me.

I wouldn't have written you this poem

I wouldn't have written you this poem
but when I knew that
you didn't want our child
it was too late for a safe abortion.

I wouldn't have written you this poem
but once I'd suckled it
I couldn't give it up
for adoption.

I wouldn't have written you this poem
but once I saw that
it reminded me of you
I just purely loved it
(impurely, too).

Who but a child?

This is a poem about the letters I wrote
that were never answered
wrote from my inmost self
again & again,
taking risks that seemed Deeper than Death;
recoiling in terror
only later.

& then of the Waiting
& the dreams that fell day after day
one dry husk after another
though I prayed for an answer
swift & daring & electric
as my question:
if not noW, When?

Who but a child would think
day will never dawn again
for her?

Who but a child would cry
Light! Light! Light!
with the intensity of her first Word.

The touch of your hand

The touch of your hand
so much gentler
than the heaviness of its absence,
sheer as the air
after a downpour.
I am ponderous as a bear,
excitable, nervy
dull
because I don't know when
I am not even waiting
for the rain
on my skin
which has forgotten.
I don't know when,
what it is
even to be in the same room,
forgotten
the rain,
breathing in the same room.
I don't know when.
I am not even waiting
not even breathing,
in the same room.
The touch of your hand
is unimaginable.

The first night of Hanukkah

Light to my light
& darkness to my darkness;
light to my darkness
& darkness to my light.

Somewhere in a room I have never been
a light flickers to life
under your strong, tender fingers.
Do you cup your hands around the flame
till it takes hold,
reflected in your eyes?

At the same moment
or a moment before or after,
under my fingers,
in a room you can only imagine,
a light—does it answer, or beckon?
finds life.

It is only the first night of Hanukkah
but faith that light
will be added to light
sustains us.

The second night of Hanukkah

Joy gathers,
under my fingers,
under yours.
I turn from lighting
the second candle
to see the two flames reflected
in the glass over the large iris
on the wall across from the small white
marble fireplace,
on the mantel of which
the menorah sits.
Its deep blue & purple petals
are illumined
by a shower of white light
from within.
I take a seat on the couch under it,
the pillows with the embroidered
Indian cloth with little mirrors,
that I sewed on the covers,
then showed you,
all about me.
Shared memory is sweet.

The third night of Hanukkah

I can no longer separate
the third smile you gave me
from the second, or the first.
Would that your hand covered mine,
lighting the third candle
together.
Still, our voices touch.
I remember how I removed from my eyes
my glasses,
& you the glasses from yours,
& your gaze met mine,
mine yours.
The beauty of it.

The fourth night of Hanukkah

The comfort
of growing used
to this gesture.
My hand is steadier.
& yours.
Light added to light.
The past, the present, the future.
Spring, & Summer, & Autumn & Winter
you greet me.
We've been together in every season.
Your faded blue jacket
over the back of the chair I sat in.
My pen in your hand
as you went about your rounds.
Your name on my lips
as I light every candle.

The fifth night of Hanukkah

Five fingers on your hand.
Five fingers on mine.
My hand clasps the pen
which inscribes these words
from my heart.
Yours holds this paper tonight,
on which glow five lights.
Dream that your hand
clasps mine.

The sixth night of Hanukkah

I light the first light,
remembering when I met you.
Your face was still bearded.
From that first moment you bent
your attention to me,
something deep in me
gave me to trust you.

I light the second light,
remembering when you removed your beard.
Your face so fresh & sun-lit
& vulnerable,
I was speechless before it.
You wore the blue shirt
that so well adorns you.
How could I tell you
what was in my heart?
I wanted to stay,
& gaze & gaze at you.
I left that day
trembling that I was permitted to hold
heaven in my eyes,
& walking carefully
as though I could lose it.

I light the third light,
remembering how,
as I struggled with my coat
with the ripped lining,
you lifted it from me
& wrapped warmth around me.

As I light the fourth light,
I remember walking proudly beside you,
your stride & mine matching,
as though you were born King, & I Queen.

Surefooted in the love of God
from whom, in whom
we can never be separated.

I light the fifth light
remembering the laughter between us
like an umbrella of lights from fireworks
rising into the air
& descending, the spray of a fountain
drenching us with glitter
as we splashed each other.

As the sixth light is kindled,
I want to speak
what I always remember—
that love & life & light
are God-given,
& I kneel in my heart;
without God's help,
how should we ever
have found each other?

The seventh night of Hanukkah

I write these Hanukkah poems for you
in the seventh month of the year,
day eleven,
knowing that the love
which composed them
will not dim.
From a country inn in the north
sunlight comes through the window.
I sit at the cloth-covered plank table
where I have lit one green candle.
An armful of wild white daisies
with golden centers
sprays out of a vase beside me.
I bring you these flowers from summer.
It is noon & there is honeycomb
from the round box before me
to spread on the bread at your table
this evening in December,
as memories
of the light in your eyes
sweeten my days & nights.

The eighth night of Hanukkah

Because of my love for you
there is no place in my being
that light is not lit.
I come to you in a white dress,
wearing a wreath of evergreen
in my hair,
on which all the candles are lighted.
In Sweden on the 13th day of December,
Santa Lucia's Day,
the daughter of the household appears
with a tray of steaming coffee, & cakes,
summoning the day
with feasting.
See, at last I have become her.
She is within me.

Dream Landscape

We were sitting in two chairs
in the middle of a vast empty classroom
where the twilight was coming irrevocably down
like a sheet of rain
or a violet wash of watercolor.
You rose, saying "I must go."
I said, "I just want to tell you . . ."
& we had a moment, only a moment
more together.
There was a deep sadness
the sadness in the face of death
as the twilight came down.
As I woke, a train, a long train
was wailing over & over again
as it went its way
through the night.
Unspeakable ache. Unspeakable melancholy.
Panic welled up in me,
a tidal wave,
& then subsided:
this is not something that will happen now,
all at once.
We have more work to do,
more work to do together.
You have taken my hands,
you are holding them in yours,
gently as baby birds.
Nevertheless,
Autumn, then Winter is coming
Night is falling.

You capture my hands

You capture my hands
like little wild birds
& hold them so tenderly

Your face is like the hewn stone
of sculptured hills

Your arms are my refuge.

The crosshatch of lines
on the back of your neck
so dear

& I love your unsuddenness

how loving you smoothes away
my fears

I long for your footstep
& your voice in my ear . . .

I have not yet begun
the feast of your eyes:
not looked directly in them
nor held them in mine . . .

It seems to me they must hold
every color of the rainbow.

I only know that their gaze
is a mirror
in which I feel beautiful
in which I can open,
a trusting flower.

Your eyes are like a river of blue iris

Li Po watched a waterfall plunge
to the river
& thought the Milky Way
had tumbled from the ninth height
of heaven

When I looked into your eyes
blue so blue
above that blue sweater
I thought the sky had tumbled from the heavens
& my heart plunged like a waterfall
in my breast

Then I read about the iris garden
on the grounds of the Meiji Shrine:
"a river of color—blue, purple & white iris
standing with their feet in water."[1]
Your eyes are like a river of blue iris
standing with their feet
in my heart.

---

[1] Burton Watson, *Chinese Lyricism, Shih Poetry from the Second to the Twelfth Century*, with translations (New York: Columbia University Press, 1971), p.146

When you & I speak to each other

It doesn't seem to matter
what we talk about
when you & I speak to each other,
what words are spoken,
what we are describing,
what we are telling each other.
There is a making music of our voices,
say tenor & contralto,
say gladness in this chance
for our voices to meet & join,
for our speech to alternate,
each taking a turn at saying
& then at listening,
or both voices tumbling out together
in a rush, one over the other in a waterfall.
There is an almost hidden laughter
at the unexpected joy of meeting.
Do you suppose everyone
hears & knows?

Honeymoon days

My favorite sin,
Lingering in the bed
this cool first of September
after a hot, humid, brutal summer.
This cool first of September
I wake to drink in the iced-tea air
& to snuggle under my soft warm blue blanket,
one arm out of the covers
to stroke the soft tortoise-shell fur
of my cat.

I wake & sleep to wake again.

One of my bosses would take off honeymoon days
when her husband returned from a business trip.

Today, cool weather returns,
& I take a honeymoon day till noon
with my companions:
cool air, warm blanket, loving cat,
& scarcely a thought in my head.
I am "sensible," into my senses,
& it is so delicious,
sinning.

Weeks-end

How sweet to own two days
a stolen week-end
with a forbidden lover, myself,
sipping mountain rhine wine
soft, fruity, semi-dry
with character & flavor
somewhat like my own . . .
I'm new at loving myself,
shy, a little clumsy,
almost afraid to know & ask
for what I want,
almost afraid to want . . .
Yet if I give to her, who needs of me,
I receive increase.

I know her already,
yet her mystery deepens . . .
I love her slender wrists & feet
the gentle searching of her touch
her moods which surprise me,
her reticence & loud laughter . . .
I accept her almost before
she reveals herself . . .
We have known each other
in many lifetimes
Caught glimpses of each other
in mirrors
Brushed against each other
down many streets
Gone off with other lovers . . .

Her lips part, & I breathe in . . .
Her blood warms with the wine,
& I respond . . .
I bathe her, feed her grapes

& suck them back into my mouth . . .
I run my fingers through her hair
& I enter her again & again
like a slow drumbeat

& I love her.
Even so.
I love her.

God makes love to me

It was a dream . . . & more than a dream.
God was making love to me in a theater.
God was a presence like the wind,
the Wind of the Spirit.
I was surrounded by bedclothes,
sheets & blankets & a quilt.
They lifted off from me & took on
a life of their own, swirling & caressing me,
gently overwhelming,
raising passion in me.
A wind animating sheets on a clothesline
on a gusty day.
The wind catching the sails of a boat
& directing its way.
I tried to take over & make love to myself,
my way, but the Spirit took over
& I let It have Its way with me.

I was on a stage.
My eyes were closed
as though I were Psyche
made love to by Eros,
the bridegroom she must not see.
Then I opened my eyes & caught an eye
in the audience.
A shyness came over me:
how much had the audience seen?

With this question in mind
I returned to the stage
for the next act,
my eyes fluttering open,
then closing,
then opening again.

Gratitude to Sophie

Dear Sophie,

Till I talked with you last night,
I was in the Slough of Despond.
Then you & I talked about Buddhism
& a good emptiness,
& how the best thing was to let feelings
float by, like clouds in a blue sky,
not grasping, never grasping.
You did not presume to give me advice,
or judgment. We simply had a conversation.
I went to sleep with the cool hand of your voice
on my brow,
waking to a long blissful dream
about sweeping up sawdust &
I forget what else,
sweeping over & over the floor
of the goat barn in Yellow Springs, Ohio,
where I lived with my first husband,
& enjoying the act of sweeping,
with sunlight pouring all around me
through the windows.
This morning, when I accepted the sun
& agreed to open my eyes to a new day,
I accomplished with ease tasks
I hadn't been able to touch before,
& I knew all over again
the meaning of gratitude.

Lunch á trois

It was a warm day for winter,
not quite February
though the thermometer read 50 degrees.
A little cool for eating outdoors,
so you & I, Hilary,
wound up with our lunches in the Citicorp building
sitting on 2 wire-backed chairs
pulled up to the low granite wall
of the semi-tropical garden I'd hardly recognized as real.
My attention wasn't exactly anywhere,
just browsing as we chewed,
when a tiny ant appeared on the ledge,
bearing a crumb of my corn bread on its back.

Whereupon you exclaimed,
"There's life in the Citicorp building!"
& we intently watched the progress
of our little guest,
going round in seemingly ineffective circles.
Our conversation resumed,
I took another spoonful of chili
& you a couple bites of sandwich
& a sip of coffee.
We had decided that perhaps the slow progress
of our ant friend
mirrored our impatience with daily life,
when a motion on the granite wall
again caught our attention.
Three, no, four ants scouting for corn bread crumbs.
Somehow our ant's circular dance
had summoned the tribe.
Alas, only one last crumb
which, in the role of Fate,
I thrust in the path of ant number 2,
as God-like we rose to our feet
& carrying our lives on our shoulders
exited the garden.

For Joan, on having laryngitis

You called me on the phone
in a whispery voice.
Before I knew it
I was whispering too.
We were a couple of kids,
co-conspirators.
Our phones were a couple of tin cans
with wire strung between them,
& we lived just across the street
from each other,
whispering secrets from our parents,
from our sisters,
from other friends,
from anyone in the universe
we didn't want to hear us.
What we had to say was so important.
Remember, what we have to say
is so important
maybe we should always whisper
to each other.

Dining *toute seule* (all alone) at Volare's

All Souls Day 1998

for Dorothy McConnell

All Soul's Day, nine years after your death,
maybe I'm finally ready to say good-bye to you,
best friend of my fifth decade,
when you were already in your eighth.
Tonight I'm saying good-bye for you
to Volare's, on West 4th Street,
with a dinner of linguine al pesto
("What's the name of that green stuff?"
you'd always ask) & good Italian bread
& a white wine spritzer with a touch of cassis,
& a small cannoli for dessert, a wee cup of espresso,
& not to forget, the inevitable cap of the evening,
sambuca. They brought so much sambuca, I needed
a doggie bag to take it home in, so I pulled out
my bottle of spring water from my purse,
& doctored it up á la anisette.

Last week, with friend Earl, I said goodbye for you
to Monte's on MacDougal Street, where you used to go
back when it was a speakeasy during Prohibition times,
& the proprietor always insists on kissing the ladies' hands,
much to your disgust. I said goodbye for you there
with zabaglione & strawberries for dessert,
which we had many a time together.
Earl, of course, reminded me that you died the same day
& the same year as Bette Davis,
& the same day of the year as Anwar Sadat.

I started out this poem thinking to say goodbye to you, for you,
but now I am thinking of saying hello & hello & hello.

To my therapist on letting go
a patient into the world

for Michael Wells, Ph.D.

Be for this 56-year-old fledgling
the great shadow of mother-father kindness
in her heart,
helping her seek out happy situations,
giving her spine in troubled times,
helping her be to others
what you have been to her.

Sometimes to stand tall,
sometimes to bend,
sometimes to feint & dodge,
deliver a well-placed blow.
To blend like a lizard
with moss-covered log or gray stone.
To flee, to flow, to fly.
To come home, to be home.

Words of thanks

for Michael Wells, Ph.D.

Steady rock in the center of a swirling stream.
Witness to the realness of what happens,
what happened
to me.

The fresh water
in which I grew roots;
the earth which clasped them.

A shade tree, green & gallant
on the dusty highway of my days,
memory of a shade tree,
anticipation
of a shade tree further along the way.

Leafy sanctuary from the pounding hotness
of summer sun burning down through the roof of the sky,
& at the other end of the year
a dense evergreen
breaking winter winds.

Time:
Father time, brother time, friend time
time to be heard
time to rest
time to think
time to learn
Time to take my time.

From knowing you
Time has become my friend.

That room is still there

(for Michael Wells, Ph.D.)

That room is still there
in which I learned
to be kinder to myself,
to "lighten up."

& the chair in which I sat
& the chair from which you rose
to greet me or to say goodbye
for the week, for the evening,
for the years.

& the corner coat rack
it took me so long to discover,
where I hung my raincoat in summer
& woollen coat in December.

The giant-sized tissue box
from which I would take
"one for the road"
when I had a sorrow or cold.

That room I have learned
how to go to,
how to leave,
how to re-create.

For Dujo Grubiŝić, Healer

Your mind,
shining its flame
into the darkness, the deeps
of mine.

Your hands,
reaching into the dark pool
of my mind,
bringing up old pain,
thrashing,
slippery as a trout,
into daylight
where it gleams,
vanquished
& at last transformed,
redeemed.

She's me!

Falling head-over-heels in love
with the child in myself.
Riding her high on my shoulders,
swinging her, swinging her,
letting her bury her head in my lap,
letting her race ahead of her cautious mother
watching her climb, climb
with my heart pounding in my mouth.
Letting her gaze her fill,
nose pressed against the glass
of every shop window.
Laughing with her as she cries, "More, More":
"Of course, child, I too want More
More of all that delights me!"
Rolling with her over & over
down grassy slopes,
digging with her in the sand,
scooping out lakes & raising castles.

Helping her fingerpaint with the tints & perfumes
on my dressing table,
peering through keyholes beside her
teetering, too, in high heels,
stuffing her dress with pillows
to see what she'll look like pregnant,
stuffing her mother's bra with kerchiefs,
Stealing out of her room in the night
to raid the refrigerator,
leaving spills & smears & fingerprints
& vehemently denying it.
Prowling in the dark of the night
to ease her fears
about what happens
when the lights go out,
what lives
when the lid of day is shut.

She's stomping through puddles,
lifting her face to the sun & rain,
tasting the wind.
Swishing through autumn leaves,
tracing her name in the steam
on winter windows.
I'm head-over-heels in love with her,
& she's me!

Karen, I love you . . .

Karen, I love you . . .
For being a trippy, flippy dame
& one of the most solid people I know . . .
For your ineffable bawdy innocence,
for your sense & nonsense,
your plain talk & your multi-colored embroideries,
your primate chatter & your fathomless silences,
your *sturm und drang*
& your sense of the sublimely ridiculous.
Are you flowing or spasmodic,
serene or irascible,
reckless or a caution,
irrational or most reasonable,
Socratic or merely erratic?
You're infuriating! I'd like
to unmask you, once & for all.
But just when I think I've done it,
I'm done with you,
You appear in another guise &
I see I'll never undress you entire,
never possess you
nor quite understand you . . .
I can only throw up my hands
& call you
Changing woman.

Who are my lovers?

... the lanky woman at the subway entrance,
with her 5-year-old son, who gently takes the shopping bags
from my hands, & matter-of-factly carries them
down the steps for me ...

... & the man with 2 school-age daughters
who reaches out his hand to steady my stumbling feet
as I get on the crosstown bus, & then, as I leave,
supports my elbow with a hand extended
like that of a male ballet dancer
supporting a danseuse ...

... the physiotherapist who carefully, confidently
takes my painful knee in his practised hands,
& pushes & prods & kneads it
as though he were making a beautiful loaf of bread
from a mound of dough,
till it moves smoothly & painlessly as I rise,
amazed, to my feet ...

... my cat who cries out how she missed me
as I open the door to my house & enter it
after a day away in the city, & then
runs to get sweet revenge
by tearing apart the twine body of my footstool
till it hangs in shreds ...

"Shall we dance?"

I often ask cab drivers, "Where are you from?"
This one asks, "Where do you think?"
I say "India or Pakistan."
He says, "You're dancing close."
I say, "Bangladesh"
He says, "You're still dancing close."
I ask "Nepal?"
He says I'm still close.
Then finally admits,
"It's a small group of islands off the coast of the mainland,
called the Maldives."
At some point he teases me, saying
"Do you think I'm attractive?"
I answer quite honestly, "Yes, very."
I ask, "Do you have family here?"
He says, "Now I do, a family of two,
You & me."
I say, "Ah the family of man."
He is silent.
I say, "The family of humankind."
"Yes," he says, "Now you've got it.
If only we all recognized that!"
Arriving at my destination,
I say, "Thanks for the dance!"
almost forgetting
to reach for my cane.

Two glad faces

I meet another cab driver in December 2004.
Hearing his accent, I inquire, as I often do,
where he is from originally.
He says, proudly, Africa.
I ask if he has heard that an African woman,
Wangari Muta Maathai,
was just awarded the 2004 Nobel Peace Prize.
He had not heard.
He is glad.

I tell him everything I know.
She is the first environmentalist,
& the first African woman, a Kenyan,
to win this prize.
She holds a doctorate in biology.
She started out planting just one tree
in her own yard.
She began.

She had asked herself, "What do we need?"
The answer came to her:
We need clean drinking water.
We need firewood.
We need nutritious food.
We need wood to build shelter.
Wars start over resources.
We should think not postwar, but prewar.
& she began.

Maathai mourned the loss of forests,
the depleted topsoil
& the fertilizer-contaminated rivers.
So she began Kenya's Greenbelt Movement.
She began tree nurseries.
She joined with the National Council of Women of Kenya,
& gave encouragement & resources to women
all over East Africa.

She was persecuted by the corrupt government
of former President Daniel arap Moi.
She was attacked & imprisoned.
Defiantly, she signed the police report
in the red of her own blood.
By now Wangari Maathai is responsible
for planting 30 million trees.
On hearing she won the Peace Prize,
she walked outside,
& in her home town of Nyeri,
in the shadow of Mount Kenya,
she planted an indigenous tree,
a Nandi flame tree, which,
when it flowers with red blossoms,
resembles a flame.

Some people were reluctant to have the Peace Prize given
to an environmentalist,
but as long ago as 1971,
Peace Prize Winner Willy Brandt had declared:
"As long as hunger exists, peace cannot prevail."

Back in the New York City cab,
when I said goodbye to the driver,
there were two glad faces
turned toward the new year.

Sources: *NPR's Renee Montagne talks with Maathai*
       BBC News
       PBS Channel 13, *Behind the Headlines*, Bonnie Erbe

Conversation with a taxicab driver

It is a Saturday in December in New York City,
at the end of the year 2004.
I am on my way to a meeting of my women artists group,
Women on the Edge.
I ask the cab driver where he is from originally.
He says, "Africa."
I ask him which country.
He says, "The Sudan."
I say, "Such sad things are happening there."
I say or he says or we both say together,
"Murder & rape of women & burning down villages"
"He says, "Yes, it is genocide."
I say, "My country should be doing more to help."
"Yes," he says, "& so should the UN."
I say that I have been writing letters,
& that I pray for the Sudan every night.
He says he sends money every week to help.
He says, "Last week 12 members of my family were murdered."
I say, "Oh My God," & "It is so hard to part
even when it is a natural death."
The tears are streaming down my face,
which has collapsed.
He looks at me & his face softens.
It is so open & vulnerable.
After I pay my fare with a generous tip
which seems not enough,
our eyes take leave of each other.
We gave each other our hearts.
It is so hard to part.

I hailed a cab today

I hailed a cab today
at Fifth Avenue & 20th Street.
When I asked to sit in front
the driver said "Sure,
I have a small cab but a big heart."
He looked like a Zorba the Greek,
but was from Algiers.
We talked about Albert Camus,
& his books, *The Plague* & *The Stranger*.
How he was the only French Nobel Prize winner,
& how he died in a car accident.
My driver told me his car struck the wall of a cemetery,
& he was buried on the other side of the wall.
We parted friends, I & this cab driver
with the big heart,
who hugged me with his warm words
& the ivory teeth of his wide smile.

June 1968

The first day warm enough to shed our coats,
walk unencumbered.
                    ROBERT KENNEDY'S SHOT
The news reverberates. Suddenly shivering
everyone puts on the labelled garment of their hate.

Transistor radios pursue us relentlessly
closing in on the assassin's identity—
it was not what most of us had bargained for.
Avoiding the mirror we strip ourselves of our thwarted hate
leave it hanging, thick, a shroud in the air.

The death and its ceremonies done
Flags wave at full mast
and when we speak of violence
we deplore the christs that spring
stubborn as weeds
from our carefully cultivated soil:
Bearded, they burn their draft cards
hurl dollars from the rafters of the Stock Exchange
Give us clean shaven men who will render to Caesar
          SHAVE THEM   SHAVE THEM

Across the world our crusade continues, our holy war . . .

I hold my small son in my arms;
brace as he twists against me in his pain.
To take on the agony of even one other proves dangerous;
it merges with the film flash of a man dying in Los Angeles,
with the photograph branded in memory of a child
lying napalmed in a Vietnamese manger . . .
like 20th century angels of the Lord, the cameramen decree that we
shall feel the rending of the outraged earth
. . . the pain enlarges to embrace the world.

Iraq, May 2004
Abu Ghraib

My countrymen, my countrywomen
are involved in horrible tortures
of human beings whose "sin" is that of
defending their own homes,
their mosques,
their own country.

We torture captives in Guantanomo Bay,
in Afghanistan & Iraq
hoping for impunity because they are not imprisoned
within the boundaries of our own country.

But we do the same to the men & women
in our own country's prisons.

Whether I look at the photographs of these evil doings
or avoid them
their deeds fill my consciousness.
I sit meditation, hoping for peaceful mind
but can't shake off the knowledge
of such brutality.

I pay taxes,
I don't raise my voice loud enough,
I am not innocent.
I am complicit.

I believe I am safe.
No one is safe
so long as we think someone else
is the enemy.

Alas, this is only a poem.

Dear God: Send dreams to George W. Bush

"Everybody talkin' 'bout going to Heaven
ain't goin' there, Heaven, Heaven"
                African American Spiritual

"One thing thou lackest: go thy way, sell whatsoever thou hast,
and give to the poor, and thou shalt have treasure in heaven . . .
how hard is it for them that trust in riches to enter into the kingdom of God!
It is easier for a camel to go through the eye of a needle,
than for a rich man to enter into the kingdom of God
                New Testament, King James version, Mark 10:21, 24-25.

Dear God: Send dreams to George W. Bush,
1001 dreams like the 1001 stories of Scheherazade,
good dreams & bad, good dreams & nightmares.
Send dreams of the earth. Let him dream the dream I dreamed,
where I was alternately walking on the earth & becoming
the earth walked upon. Let him shudder in his sleep
as he imbibes chemicals & poisons that permeate the soil.
Let him soar in the sky like an eagle, & sit on the eagle's nest,
hatching young ones, & pray for their future.
Let him become a fish, a dolphin, a whale to swim first in cool clear water,
& then in the now radioactive seas, & feel the difference. Let him be
bombarded in the depths of the ocean by sonar & wake troubled & confused,
swimming in circles & no longer knowing where to go or how to be.
Let him dream he is one tree in an ancient grove, chopped down
with his brothers & sisters, screaming under the saw.

Then let him dream of peace, a peace that is even more than the absence
    of war.
Let him dream that he sits in an American Indian tribal council,
where the tribe carefully, cautiously plans to leave the earth & the skies
& the seas unpolluted for seven generations.
Let him see how the women of the tribe remove from office
the men who do not honor this tradition.
Instead of throwing stones,
let him become in his dreams the Indian boy
who handles stones reverently,

121

who keeps a precious stone in his pocket,
a symbol of a bond with the earth,
who only hunts for what he & his tribe need,
& first in prayer asks permission
of the animal whose life is being sacrificed.
Let him be the chief who plans a big Giveaway, a Potlatch,
with all his precious possessions distributed to the entire tribe,
thereby gaining spiritual stature.

Let him be first the Afghan bride & bridegroom,
& then the Iraqi bride & bridegroom
whose weddings were bombarded by American bombs,
who never had a wedding night.
& the musicians & relatives at those weddings.
Let him be them one by one,
& then wake to realize the horror of war,
Let him be Saddam Hussein,
another man who abused his power,
& wake to find himself caught
crouching in a hole in the earth.

Let him be Abraham Lincoln in one dream,
his heart torn apart by the deaths of his countrymen,
& let him be then Walt Whitman, nursing fallen soldiers
& writing poems of anguish for his fallen leader.
Let him in a dream carry a child in his belly for nine months,
giving birth like a woman & nursing babies at his breast,
learning how precious life is.

Let him dream how it feels to be among the wretched of the earth.
Let him be born a Haitian, an Afghan, an Iraqi,
with all his possessions destroyed, & his soil polluted by
American radioactive tanks & weapons.
Let him be born a Palestinian, whose family has been homeless
for three generations.

Let him feel how it is to have friends he didn't have to buy,
& to be a small neighborhood shopkeeper
at the mercy of corporations.

May God stretch his heart open with dreams,
like Joseph in the Old Testament, like Mary in the New,
like those God has chosen.

Let him sleep on the grass on a summer night, looking up at the stars,
with a clear conscience, & let him know in every fiber of his being
how that feels.

Let him honor his name & his family & his country & Earth itself.
Let him honor the Universe.

Dear God: Send George W. Bush dreams.

"A Disease Called Owning"

Reflections on Dick Cheney's record

"The Hopi believe that when they first came to these mesas untold years ago, the land was empty save for one humble farmer, a man they call Massau. He taught the Hopi how to survive here, says Masayesva, and he warned them about dangers ahead. He said, 'There are others who are coming. It will be a very short time before they arrive. They're not going to ask; they'll take. With each step, they'll say, 'This is mine.' They have a disease called owning. With every step they will claim the land. They'll claim the water, the air. They will think they are gods.' Our ancestors asked him, 'How big is your land?' He said, 'This is not my land. I only take care of it.' Then he made a circle with his hand to indicate the earth. 'This is what I'm taking care of. I'm not a god. I'm a farmer.'" [1]

This man, as the natives say,
speaks with forked tongue.
This man engineered war on Iraq,
and then gave lucrative reconstruction contracts,
without the required bidding competition, to
Halliburton, the corporation which hired him as vice president,
which still pays him $150,000 a year in
"deferred compensation" [2]
There is an historical name for men (or women)
who do such things: Robber Barons,
who act out of individual & corporate Greed.
There is another name: War Profiteers.

How did he help get us into this war?
By stacking intelligence against Iraq,
controlling key positions in the State Department,
lying about Saddam Hussein's "weapons of mass destruction."
lying about Saddam's supposed connection with Al Qaeda. [3]
This man plays Santa Claus to the rich,
while letting the underclasses pay for his war.

---

[1]   Folger, Tim, "A Thirsty Nation," in *oneearth*, Fall 2004

[2]   Allman, T.D., "The Curse of Dick Chaney," in *Rolling Stone*, September 16, 2004

This man, though war-thirsty, voted against
funding for the Veterans Administration.[4]
Voted against protective gear for our soldiers in Iraq.
He puts our youth, our men & women,
in harm's way, & then refuses to care for the wounded,
the widows.
This man believed he was exempt from fighting our country's wars—
he finessed 5 draft deferments. [5]
Others could fight, could risk their lives.
Who? You guessed it: the middle class, the working class.

Would you buy a used war from this man?
2 wars, 3 wars, a war that will never end in our lifetime?

What kind of a war? A war that uses radioactive tanks,
not only polluting the soil of Iraq, but sowing cancers in our own soldiers,
sowing cancers in their children to be.
When we do, or permit, such evil,
it comes home to rest for generations.

This man does not love our land—the soil, the water, the air.
He fought efforts to clean up hazardous waste
& backed tax breaks for energy corporations.[6]
This man is part of an Administration
which rewards timber lords for decimating our forests.

Neither does this man love humanity.
This man opposed extending the Civil Rights Act,
& opposed the release of Nelson Mandela in South Africa . . . [7]

He is not interested in workplace safety,
but longer hours & less job security
for the underclasses.

---

[3]   Ibid

[4]   Ibid

[5]   Ibid.

[6]   Ibid

[7]   Ibid

He would gamble social security in the stock market,
amputate sections of our Bill of Rights,
push the Middle-East toward all-out war,
& legalize torture.

People the world over suffer from this man
who suffers from "a disease
called owning."

Dreamt about war

Dreamt about war.
Dreamt about shoes, battered empty shoes,
men's & women's & children's.
About mud-encrusted piles of clothing,
rolls of shirts, of jackets, of trousers.
Boxes of battered books & photographs.
For some reason a box of John Lennon's family photographs.

& herded hungry animals,
lean, starved dogs.
& hats, khaki hats, denim hats.
Bales of used clothing.
Bales of discarded newspapers,
read & unread,
words & headlines & photos with staring eyes.

Bodies; men taking guns that were still usable
from bodies.
Teeth that would never chew again,
arms without hands,
legs without feet,
heads with staring eyes.

Fields burnt to the ground, foodless fields.
A book with pictures of a father & child.
Empty staring eyes, dead eyes,
horror-filled alive eyes.

& radios & TV's, battered,
with voices coming out of them,
standing there,
not in anyone's room,
anyone's living space.

Dreamt about war.

"The Same Fate as the Poor"[1]

December 2005

In Memoriam
Sr Maura Clarke, Sr Ita Ford, Jean Donovan, Sr Dorothy Kazel

On the twenty-fifth anniversary of the rape & murder of 3 Catholic nuns &
1 Catholic laywoman in El Salvador

"I am trying more and more to deal with the social sin of the first world. It's not an easy question.[2]
—Jean Donovan

"The work is really what Bishop Romero called 'acompañamiento' (accompanying the people)[3]
—Sister Maura Clarke

"Several times I have decided to leave El Salvador. I almost could except for the children, the poor, bruised victims of this insanity. Who would care for them? Whose heart could be so staunch as to favor the reasonable thing in a sea of their tears and loneliness? Not mine, dear friend, not mine.[4]
—Jean Donovan in a letter to a friend about two weeks before she died.

"I remember when she was getting ready to leave and had to pack . . . I noticed she had a couple of pieces of Waterford crystal in there, and I said, 'Oh, how neat—you carry this with you.' Because usually you . . . save it for company coming—and I think that's what Jean did with her life—she didn't save it for when company comes; it was meant to be used; you didn't get too cautious with it; it had to be filled to the brim, not saved for later on, or for special company.[5]
—Pat de Angelis

---

[1] Title of Sr Judith Noone's book, *The Same Fate as the Poor*
[2] Carrigan, Ana, *Salvador Witness: The Life and Calling of Jean Donovan*, Orbis Books, Maryknoll, NY c1984, 2005
[3] Ibid.
[4] Ibid.
[5] Ibid.

What was their crime?
Feeding & binding up the wounds of the poor;
transporting them to safe places,
teaching them nutrition,
comforting them.
Witnessing.
They came to teach & they learned to learn,
finally, the same fate as those they served.
I don't want to rehearse again
the last moments
of their lives on this earth.

I just want, trembling, tentatively,
to think about their sisters,
about those who prepared their cast-off bodies
for burial.
This is task enough.

There must always be gratitude
that the remains of martyrs can be found
& handled, at last, reverently.
Their sacred garments for work,
their habits—blue jeans—which Salvadoran peasants
pulled back on their bodies to give them cover,
one of these on backwards.
These muddied blue jeans eased off the four bodies.
The bathing of the dear bodies
for their last rites,
by their sisters, with the love of new mothers,
with the love of fresh widows.
Undoing the desecration as best they can.
Soaping then rinsing, then drying their hair,
which seems still alive.
Closing the lids of those eyes which saw with horror the last moments
of each self & her sisters, then kissing them tenderly.
Handling with care & pouring water, sacred water,
over every inch of their bodies.
Kissing their foreheads, their palms
& the back of their hands.

Kissing their feet.
& then dressing them as their mothers
had dressed them as children,
but this time for burial.

I imagine Dorothy, Ita, Jean & Maura
shorn of these earthly bodies,
walking together into the Light,
into that place where there is rejoicing
over their lives,
given for Christ, given for the many.
Into that place where there is Thanksgiving,
& no more pain.

Piercings

Riding on the PATH train from New York to New Jersey,
I see again, am forced to see, a young woman with piercings
in her tongue, her upper lip, wherever.
She is thrusting out her tongue & moving it over her lips
as though to remind herself, continually, of the deed she has done.
I wince when I think of the pain she inflicted on herself,
& how many young people are doing, have done, the same.

I imagine myself surrounded by a circle of the young,
all with such piercings.
I ask the question,
"Why have you injured yourselves?"
Like a Greek chorus they cry out,
"The whole Earth is injured,
& thousands have died in Afghanistan & Iraq,
our women & men among them . . .
Citizens, soldiers, rescue workers, rebuilders.
animals, flowers, trees, water, earth, air
& so we too, we too, something is injured,
Something is dying, in us, in you."

You've given words to my long ago

(On reading Diana Abu-Jaber's novel, Crescent)

You've given words,
you've given breath,
you've given song
to my long ago,
to how I wanted to be loved
but couldn't imagine.

You've given words,
you've given breath,
you've given song
to my anguish
at how my country has bombed,
has tortured,
has taken possession by force
of smaller countries,
of Arab countries,
of Latin American countries,
of Asians,
of Africans
all over this world.

You've given words,
you've given breath,
you've given song
To how my country has consorted
with the ruthless, the evil ones,
who took land, who took food,
who took the clothing off the backs
from those they belonged to.

Who took food out of the mouths of babes
& milk out of the breasts of mothers
& blood out of the very stones,
who took the bread & the wine & the oil.

How can I bear that I & my countrymen,
countrywomen, are living off the lifeblood
of those who should have inherited the land
that was in their families for generations.

How can I bear the sweetness of love
in my life,
knowing we have killed the lovers,
the brides & bridegrooms,
torn children from the arms of mothers & fathers,
taken the hope of grandmothers & grandfathers,
of their bloodlines continuing.
Their land, their trees, their water
polluted, destroyed.

For years after the Gulf War,
& before we formally declared war on Iraq,
bombings, embargoes, starvation,
deaths from lack of medical supplies,
deaths from radiation we left in the soil,
kept from our eyes by the American media
in collusion with our own government.

You've given words,
you've given breath,
you've given song
to hope as well as despair,
to trust as well as to suspicion,
to humor as well as passion,
to waiting & mourning
& welcoming.

You've told the stories of lovers,
of family & relatives & guests,
of magical characters,
of cruel despots, of artists & poets,
of scholars.

The sumptuous stories of foods & exotic spices,
of plenty, of more than enough to eat,
of fruits & vegetables & meats,
of rice & other grains,
of sauces & gravies & omelettes
& salads & candies & sweet desserts,
of oil & vinegar,
of bread,
of wine.

May the stories of love & lovers,
of feeding each other,
triumph,
as in your novel.
In the world.

Like a child I splash

Like a child
I splash
in the bathtub
in the shower
lifting my face
as though to the rain.

But thoughts are never far
of Iraq, of Afghanistan
of the storms of sand
& water scarce,
because of the war we started
& continue,
of what our bombs destroy
so a mother, a grandmother
there
has no electricity
& infrequent water.
How should she choose,
from the little left:
water to drink,
water to wash clothes with
water to wash herself
& her family.
We make war there,
endlessly.
Because we want their oil
we take away their civilization.
Water, electric lights,
every amenity.
I want to take them in my arms,
under my shower,
into my bath;
I want to give them water for their every need,
water to cook with, water to wash with,
water to drink, water to splash in.

I want to make their lights come on,
every time they need light to read by,
light to sew by,
light to see each other's faces.

I want to give them
my everydays.

It is the first day of my 46th year.

It is the first day of my 46th year.
It is.
I do not feel young
because I remember so much
& there is much I would not forget.
Because my arms remember
husband & lover & child & friend
my arms remember & my skin remembers
touch after touch
as my feet remember
cool grass & hot-baked ground & water & pebble & stone
I do not feel young.

It is the first day of my 46th year.
It is.
It is the first day of my 46th year
& I do not feel old
because life leaps in me
like a green frog springing,
then landing again in the green grass;
life leaps in me
like my fingertips spring off the drum skin
as though they touched fire
as though they were fire,
because unborn poems leap in my womb
& my voice leaps from my throat
I do not feel old.

It is the first day of my 46th year.

Searching

It is a word I know well,
or a name or a joke or vignette,
but, like my cat,
won't come when I call it,
searching won't bring it,
so I drop it down
into the well of my heart,
& wait.
It is there, & it rises, at last,
in its own time,
to the surface of my mind,
a gift from the riches of memory.

O woman with silver hair

O woman with silver hair,
how have I become you?

O woman who walks with a cane,
how have I become you?

O woman with a grandson,
a granddaughter,
how have I become you?

O woman who has buried
a sister, a mother, a father,
how have I become you?

O woman with a long past
& shorter future,
how have I become you?
How has it happened
that I have become you?

A great man is taking leave of this world

(for Rev. Paul Abels)

A great man is taking leave of this world,
a man large in heart,
a gracious, welcoming, noble soul,
lover of all manner of things
& all kinds of people:
infant & elderly,
large & little,
outrageous, quiet,
Gay, Lesbian, Straight, Undecided.
Jew, Catholic, Methodist, Greek Orthodox, Feminist, Buddhist.

A man I call Friend, Artist, Patron, Pastor.
Father, Mother, Sister, Brother.
Walker on Water. Tightrope Balancer,
Puller of Rabbits out of Hats. Your hat & my hat.
Gifts we had not known were there.

A man who reached out both hands to the dispossessed
& fought like hell for them & against their oppressors
is taking leave of this world.
That man who when giving communion
would look into your eyes, speak your name
& say, "Given for you." Given for you, Dorothy,
Given for you, John, Bob, Martha, Tom. Given for you.
You. Louise. Gretchen. Ed, Ann, Earl, Karen.
Knowing him you knew that these words
spoke for his own life,
given gladly to the many.

A man who loved beauty is taking leave
of the beauties, the "10,000 things of this world—"
the catalpa tree, the stained glass windows,
the gleaming silver coffee service.
Paul loved to make beauty, & to drink it in.
To make music, to speak truth, to speak poetry,
to host dinners & teas & champagne breakfasts

& readings & receptions & overnight guests.
To arrange flowers from the garden or florist
& armfuls of wildflowers & grasses from the meadows,
& turn evergreen branches into Christmas wreaths
with glorious lavish crimson bows

A man named Paul Abels is taking leave of this world.
Reverend. Reverent.
Whose life was engagé, engaged in grappling with the needs of the human
community
issues of ethics & humanity,
the politics that sprang from the heart.
Ireland, Iran, Tibet, Japan, Vietnam.
Albany, Rensselaerville, Manhattan. Manhattan.

A great man is taking leave of this world.
In his last days, though speech has been taken from him,
grace abides in his presence,
& his smile of surpassing sweetness.
He speaks with his eyes
his gladness at this last meeting
& sorrow at parting.
He speaks with the still firm clasp of his hand,
warming yours & mine & those of an endless procession of guests
he still welcomes to his home
& his hospital room
in his last days & hours.
The phone rings; it is never still.
The letters come, & the cards & gifts & flowers
& the love returned & returning.

A great man is taking leave of this world,
whose name quickens in our soul like candle flame,
who will never take leave of our memory.

Julie Kurnitz's last words

On her deathbed
when asked by her sister
what she wanted,
meaning terminate life support
or not,
this consummate actress,
this comedienne, said,
"I want everything
& I want nothing."

Elegy for Betty Lord, 91,

Saturday, November 12, 2005

That cultured & effortlessly theatrical voice.
Warm, but with the kind of intonation
that would bring your soul to attention
when she called your name.
The short, fine, cropped white hair.
The carved wooden cane.
No vast wardrobe but a drawerful of special touches—
unusual beads or a scarf or a pin
that could be nobody else's . . .
Climbing the stairs to her small, austere Village apartment,
not willing to admit the increasing difficulty of it.

Always I knew I was risking my heart
loving that woman who had reached her nineties.
Knew I was going to have to say goodbye to her
before I was ready to.

Though small in stature you would never call this valiant woman delicate.
Wrote songs & poems & made small sculptures & rubbings
& sewed booklets & tried her hand at anything else
you were not expecting, like singing, like drumming,
like chanting or howling.
So modest about her work even as she shared it,
calling it a "trifle, a little bit of something."

Insomniac,
with honesty & courage she looked at the darker side of life,
even invited it.
Lately she'd quoted Gerard Manley Hopkins'
"Carrion Comfort" in a phone conversation:
"O the mind, mind has mountains; cliffs of fall
Frightful, sheer, no-man-fathomed. Hold them cheap
May who ne'er hung there."
But never think it was depressing to know her!
Soon I would get a CD in the mail with a gutsy upbeat
Broadway-worthy song she had written.

I once wrote a poem to her, speaking of
"The matter of you & me & rebirth."
It ended with ". . . it began to seem almost that simple,
the matter of dying to the past
& the little pause of Now
& then a gently expanding new breath, new birth."

After hearing you died Tuesday, peacefully,
with your cousin beside you,
in St. Vincent's Hospital, close to home,
to your Bank Street apartment,
I went out to the grocery store.
I'd been away on a trip, & meantime
the sidewalk of that block had been taken up,
taken down to the earth,
& was being repoured.
There was a yellow plastic ribbon
strung so I had to walk out in the street
to get to where I was going.

Surely you were a Zen master,
who with your energy & spunk
will be poured speedily into that rebirth
you were itching for.

As I think of you,
your soul flown,
your dear body lying on a bed in St. Vincent's,
I can almost see you transform to a new infant,
hollering your entrance back into this world.
I'll be looking for you!

Betty's gone

Do I have time to grieve, to mourn?
My body stops short, says
you'll do nothing else for now,
this day, this afternoon.
You'll think of things unsaid, undone
& tears will come.
You'll wish that, like Joan,
you had cooked in the kitchen together
many an evening,
words & thoughts coming easier
while you chopped & peeled & shredded,
or even in that common friendly silence
of woman & woman, where words unspoken
went even deeper.
You'll wish you had gotten around to sending
that new Mary Oliver poem from *The New Yorker*.
You'll wish Betty had been not quite so private,
had asked for help or favors or to be listened to,
more often,
& you'll be glad for when she did,
for when she did,
& the life she lived.

We didn't ask

So . . . death scoops up a life
from the waters
clumsily, roughly as a bear,
or delicately as a raccoon,
washing it fastidiously
before feasting on it.
Death plays with a life
like a cat its quarry
letting it go free
only to pounce on it again.
How is it
we keep stumbling
on this scene
we didn't ask
to observe,
didn't even know
to be curious about?

death comes

death comes, close-mouthed
a finger swishing hush through the air
sealinG sealinG sealinG

On Allen Ginsberg's Death at 70

Saturday, April 5, 1997

Well, he did it, the old man, the not-so-old-man,
made it through to the end of an incredible life!
A Buddhist priest interviewed by newscasters
said he'd just told Allen
that he'd lived enough for five lifetimes
in a single life.
Hadn't realized that at that infamous Chicago convention,
he'd sat cross-legged among the protestors getting clubbed left
& right by the police,
intoning OM,
& they couldn't figure out what he was doing,
so they thought they'd arrest him for "subversion!"
Hallelujah!

My mother died

My mother died
with her mouth open
like a baby bird.
When they pulled the sheet
over her face
it seemed like an infant life
was being extinguished.
Then they wrapped
her thin form,
but her feet still existed.
Anxiously, my father
covered them.

Shopping at Foodtown Market, Jersey City

the Sunday after Thanksgiving

I stood waiting at the counter
with 2 cartons of yogurt
& a special issue of *Harper's Bazaar*,
"on the fine art of holiday dressing."

The woman in front of me was,
what? 20 years older?
On her white hair was a bright pink beret
at a jaunty angle.
Her outer jacket was red violet,
& she carried a fuchsia cloth shopping bag.

I fell in love with her
as I do with every one of us
who makes the human condition
look dashing, & gallant.

& I told her I loved her colors,
how she was like a symphony to my eyes.
She drank it up. I didn't let her see
that I walked out behind her
with tears streaming down my cheeks . . .

Where is my own little mama,
her dear dwindled body laid in the ground?
Somewhere oh somewhere let her spirit be dancing,
let her hear songbirds,
& let her wear colors that sing.

My father's socks, my mother's potholder

My father's thin ribbed maroon socks
to cover & warm my feet.
My mother's red plaid flannel potholder
edged in blue,
(the one I gave her), to protect my hand from the heat,
from burning.
To these I turn
like a child grasping the corner of her blanket
for comfort.
To these I turn
when memory alone is not enough,
when I need something to touch.
Yes, they existed on this earth,
in the flesh.
Yes, they existed.
Yes.

Never

"Why should a dog, a horse, a rat, have life
And thou no breath at all? Thou'lt come no more,
Never, never, never, never, never!"
—Shakespeare, *King Lear*

Never is a piece of thread that
pulls two edges of a wound together,
then dissolves in the flesh;
its stitches won't need pulling,
ever.

Never is a broken limb
that won't require re-setting
though it might ache, sometimes,
in damp weather.

Never is the kind of bee
with a single stinger,
barbed, like a harpoon;
unlike a wasp's
it cannot be withdrawn
but its owner will not live
to sting again.

Never is an easy word:
in Shakespeare's *Lear*, even,
it tears the heart from its moorings
only five times
& seems to promise
an end to grieving.

Walking through the anniversary of your death

(for Nancy Lee, my twin)

Still buttering toast in the morning
22 years after you've gone
in a too quiet kitchen . . .

Ritually, I lift gold & red chrysanthemums
out of Great Aunt Emelia's copper teakettle
on the round oak table
to freshen them,
keep them living a little longer;
cut off dead buds & drooping heads,
snip stems on an angle
just above where they'd swollen shut
till they can again drink water.

I am a woman in her fifties
but a child was taken from the side
of me, a child,
a young woman from the side of a young woman.
We were in the womb together:
how could we have imagined existence without the other?

On this morning of the eve of your long-ago death
I walk to the bus-stop
through leaves shed like lives from the trees
feathers shed from bird wing,
keeping the season.

Waiting for the bus in the late fall chill,
children prancing by wearing Hallowe'en costumes
to school,
I see gray sky reflected in broken bits of mirror on the ground.

Eight hours at work interrupt
till I light the candle for memory at dusk,
visible flame which will lift
the weight of grief
from my heart;

flickering life which gives you life
even through the night,
which still lit
will greet tomorrow's sunrise.

At the time of the glow of autumn leaves,
every year you come back for this visit,
splashing color into my life
to help me make it through the winter.

"The Letter"

(for Nancy Lee)

Nineteen years, nearly, after your death,
I've set myself
to re-enter the space
created by our letters
to one another.
In the middle of a pile of unfolded papers
in your handwriting
is a reproduction of a painting
by Kay Fjell of Norway,
torn from an illustrated desk calendar.
The left edge is untrimmed
where a spiral of wire
once bound it into the pages of a year
sometime between 1953 and 1970.

In a room draped with orange,
in front of the white-clothed round table
by an open casement window
stand 2 young girls
in orange dresses
with grey-stockinged legs
& blue kerchiefs.

So close they stand
that the 2 orange dresses
blend into one.
With 3 hands they hold a letter,
& their heads,
joined at the crown,
are bent
to peruse it together.

A breeze
coming through the window
which looks out onto a far landscape
is visible in the white curtains

swirling into the small room.
To their right is a painted wood bench.
In a moment they will move toward it
to sit there together,
their feet knowing
the boards of the floor they stand on
so that they step sideways & turn
& bend their knees to sit
without raising their eyes
from the letter
they share together.

Their backs are toward the far landscape
out the window
as the warm orange of the room
& their twin dresses
embrace them forever.

I rise from the typewriter
& walk through the next room
into the kitchen,
where a woman's voice on the radio
completes the last phrase of a song
about red roses
which hangs in the damp air.

On this rainy 5th of July
at Paul & Thom's inn,
Catalpa House,
in Rensselaerville, New York,
Nineteen hundred & eighty-nine,
my eyes drown in the green
outside the kitchen windows.

I walk back to the parlor room
where the typewriter is set up
in front of the lace-curtained window
by a piano on which is the music
from Mendelssohn's *"Songs Without Words,"*

I look again at the page torn from your diary
twenty or thirty or more years ago.
It glows in the dim rainy daylight
of the room I sit in.
At the top of the page you've written,
"Merry Christmas, Darling!"
Christmas in July.
At the foot of the page you sign
"Love!" with one of your fanciful nicknames.

"Yes," I think, "yes,"
we stood often
so close together.

Let me not be the one

Let me not be the one
whose umbrella is still open
blocks after the rain has stopped.
Let me not be the one
whose headlights are still on
half an hour after my car
has left the tunnel.
Let me be the one who wakes early,
easily, naturally,
without the blare of an alarm clock
in my ear.
Let me not be late
at the gate of heaven.

So Long Ago, When I Was Too Young

I remember, on warm nights,
slipping out of the house,
& flinging myself down in the grass
on the breast of Mother Earth,
before I was consciously calling Her that.
I was 13, 14, 15,
& despaired of ever growing to be
a Woman of Experience.
I felt trapped in a life that was not exciting.
How could it ever be different?
I wanted to write novels,
but what was there in my life to write about?
I wanted adventure,
but didn't know where to find it.
Since the one attempt to run away from home
at age 5 or 6,
with my sister & another friend,
which we backed out of
as fast as my wise mother gave us permission,
it had never occurred to me
to do that again.
Where could I go?
Where was the mystery in existence,
the edge of danger?
Not in my small town, my small life.
I wanted to be deep,
I wanted to feel intensely.
I wanted romance.
I envied the gypsies.
I didn't know enough to be drawn to the big city,
or to the life of an artist,
which I couldn't begin to imagine.
I didn't know to be drawn to the life of the Spirit,
of which I never learned in Sunday School.
Goddess, how I hated being Too Young.

Glorying in the universe

(for Kevin, 18 months)

Something in me was holding its breath
as your mother set you down on the floor
inside my house,
a vortex of energy.

You were quick to go for the knobs on the gas stove.
We jumped to our feet
every time you headed for the kitchen.

After we grabbed the glass juicer & set it on a high shelf,
we gave you free access to the pots & pans,
preparing our ears for random crashes.
But you approached them with purpose.
Heading for the refrigerator door,
you took down the trout magnet, dropped it into a pot,
reached for a long wooden spoon, & began to cook it
on a turned over colander, like your fisherman father.

Your labors in the kitchen finished, you re-entered
the living room, & made for the piano.
Our ears prepared again for crashes.
We had seen your little body in a frenzy of energy,
shaken like a tree in a high wind;
Other children have been known to bang on a piano,
intoxicated with it as noise.

You struck a key, & *listened.*
Another, & then another.
You climbed onto the bench & sat there,
your hands poised over the keys
like some small virtuoso,
as though you knew from another life
about making music.

I was yet to visit *your* house.
When I did, a month later, I found
your father had bought you a small rake.
He showed you how to use it on the rug,
as though you were raking earth, or leaves.
After a few strokes, you raised it up
like a guitar, & began to strum it
to the rhythm of the music on the tape player.

You were in the next room
when the tape ended, with a small click;
you raced back to try
to turn it on again.

At nap time
your mother played lullaby tapes.
Alas, you got to your feet & began
to dance!

You hear the music of light & color
too. I look at the photo of you
in your yellow slicker, held aloft
in your mother's arms, glorying in
the branch of sunlit yellow autumn leaves
above you, your face aglow with wonder.

Watching you, I am a child again;
I glory; I relearn to look & listen.

Waving

Dear Grandson,
The last time I saw you,
a couple of weeks ago
you were smiling
& opening & closing your wee plump hands
as you waved them to family & friends
at your great-granddaddy's memorial gathering;
my joy, our joy in our season of grieving.

I talked with your mom today.
She said you'd been out in the yard
waving to the birds,
waving to the bumblebees,
as though they were persons,
& we giggled.

But perhaps
you're so fresh, so young
you know
that the act of a bird, a bee
waving its wings to fly
is one with the act of greeting.

Kevin's costume, Hallowe'en 2004

The Bambino, my grandson, has now aged 10 ½ years.
Each year his costume, homemade,
emerges from his own imagination.
Two years ago he was costumed as Gandalf
from Tolkien's *Lord of the Rings*,
with a long grey beard, leaning on his staff.
This year he chose to become a gladiator.
A trip to the Good Will thrift shop produced
a sleeveless grey shift of a dress, sandals,
an arm guard, & two embossed metal plates
in which he drilled holes, one for a chest guard,
the other to armor his back, held together
by long boot laces.
Garbing himself in the grey dress,
slipping it over his head, he said,
"I'm getting in touch with my feminine side."

Wee Beastie

For Amy Caitlin, 8 months

When you started out life
sleeping by Mama's & Daddy's bed,
your Dad had to move to your brother's room
to get a night's sleep—
even when you were well-fed & diapered & content,
you grunted & creaked like a squeaky door
round the clock.

Eight months later when I call your mother
on the telephone
it sounds like a whole barnyard of animals—
or is it a zoo?—
grunts, squeals, squeaks, clucks, chirps & squawks.
Is all this really only one little girl?

You seem to know you're not just human,
but a creature, a wild thing, a wee beastie.

& as though to confirm it,
now that you're traveling on all fours,
now that you're really going places,
you carry along a rattle, your 4-year-old brother's sock, whatever,
gripped in your first milk teeth
like your dog Gus carries a ball or a bone.

Just dancing around

My two-year-old granddaughter Amy
came to the phone.
"Thank you for the 'peenk' dress,
Grammie," she said.
Then there was a pause
after which I heard,
"... ju s s t d a a n c i n g a r round ..."

Kitten, when did you get to be a cat?

Kitten, when did you get to be a cat?
That first day when I chanted OM in a deep voice
you looked at me askance & went flying across the room
as though I'd hurled you.
Today, & even yesterday, you stand your ground.
One day you were little & frail, bird-boned,
yet before I knew it you were a weight to heft.
One day you walked surely along the curved rim of the bathtub
secure in your slender grace,
& the next time I noticed, you were too big to balance on that rim
& lost your footing & got one furry leg very very wet.
One day you stood on all fours to dip your mouth into your water bowl
but now you lie down on the floor to drink.
When did you get big?
I guess, like any child, little by little.

I am the cat at the window

I am the cat at the window at sunrise
& you are the songbird.
My mouth opens & closes
& strange noises come from my throat
when I try to imitate your sound.
It is true,
I want to entice you with your own language
till I can get close enough
to ruffle your feathers:
my whole being quivers
in anticipation
of tasting you.

Dear Cat

You have branded me.
You have shed dark hairs
that show on my light clothes,
light hairs that show on my dark clothes
for all to see.
I am your head of cattle,
my land is your land,
& you have marked it
with an abundance of tufts of hair,
no matter how much I brush or comb you.
I know I don't *own* you,
but I suspect that you think you own me
& you have ways of showing it
to the whole world.
Though the fourth finger of my left hand is bare,
you might as well have placed a ring on it.

I search for my cat

I search for my cat
in all her hideaways,
call & call her name.
She's not in the wardrobe
or the storage room
nor under the bedskirt.
Where?

Oh! There she is,
sitting quietly on the sofa,
in plain sight
& so, well hidden.
A look in her eye
seems to say:
"Trying to find me?
I was here all along,
like the sun & the rain."

I wish that I could clean my soul

I wish that I could clean my soul
as easily & immediately,
as you, Cherie cat,
clean your chest, your face, your feet, your belly.
A lick for unkind thoughts or words,
repeated licks for sloth,
& for deeds done or not done,
all woven into the fabric
of each day.

Or the way,
when you're not up for loving,
without a thought of guilt,
you shrug & shake my caresses away.

You, cat, & your kind,
with your rough little pink tongues,
must be among the cleanest
& most honest
of creation.

Cat & Mouse

My cat is not a killer
He is delighted to find a friend in the house
who is live & warm & moves quickly,
unpredictably,
squirms under his paw,
scurries,
requires alertness
for this game.

Why does his playmate
grow less enthusiastic
move slower & slower
& not quicken again?
Why can't he tease & shake him
back to life,
back into the game?

My cat did not know his own strength,
did not understand about big & little.
My cat did not know
about dead.

The long-legged bus driver

The long-legged bus driver
folds at the knees—
grasshopper behind the wheel

Fitting into days like blue jeans

One day fits you firm
like blue jeans that've been worn
at least once
but not often
since you washed them.
The zipper zips.
You bend, lift, sit
easily.

Another day is stiff,
resists knee-bend,
complains at the zipper.
Is acid-washed,
a corset,
a tourniquet.

Makes you want to salvage,
makes you want to patch & mend
& safety pin
& wear again
every day the universe
fits you fine.

Thunder poem

My feet secure on the ground;
thunder crashing in waves in the sky.
May the anger in my heart
be followed by the rain of compassion.

Sitting here

Sitting here
I see
strings of raindrops
linger
under the iron stair rails
as though
these clear beads
in a black-framed abacus
were there
to be counted

A moth

A moth
flying straight at me
struck my mouth softly:
a kiss from the universe.

Fortune cookie

Outside the Chinese restaurant
a little bird pecking at a fortune cookie
Should I bend & open it
for her/for him?

One yellow leaf

One yellow leaf,
an early turner
caught like a Christmas ornament
in the slender branches
of a knee-high evergreen,
a little tree,
not dense but feathery.

One yellow leaf
hung on an evergreen
the luminous green
of cat's eyes at night
when seen by day
after the rain
in a strange three-quarter light
under a watery skim milk sky.

Who needs to buy gold at a jeweler's,
who needs to buy emeralds
whose memory holds,
from a walk in the forest,
one yellow autumn leaf
& raindrops
strung in the slender branches
of a knee-high evergreen.

Forget calendar time!

Forget calendar time!
The birds have been trying to tell me
it's Spring
though the calendar says it's only March 6,
& yesterday evening
the ice cream truck
with its tinny music box sound
came strolling along the street I live on
like the Pied Piper of Hamelin.

January flowers

It was a two-hands-on-the-umbrella
North Wind January rain.
My own plum umbrella turned
inside out, its petals reaching
toward the sky
as though to drink it all in,
forgetting to give me shelter.
At the corner of Eighth Street & Greenwich
a fallen green umbrella lay,
a folded violet leaf,
its spokes like veins,
its stem resting
in a pool of water.

& all along the street
bobbed January flowers.

February day

Grey sky,
A million pinpoints of grey rain
crowd onto the window panes
as I hunger for color.

Where is a child in yolk-yellow slicker & hat
& shiny black boots
I can take by the hand
to go splashing in puddles
with an apple-green laugh
& a blue-sky umbrella

& where is the color crimson?

The lavender iris blossoms

The lavender iris blossoms
push out of their paper cocoons,
then—oh miracle!—expand their wings.

2 Stems of Purple Iris

Walking to work up that street of many colors,
6th Avenue,
through the profusion of green trees
& shrubs & cacti & potted & cut flowers—
the branches, too, of autumn's red berries—
taking over the sidewalks of the flower district,
I came upon the corner where I daily meet
one large but mellow dog,
its thick fur blond as wheatstalks,
reclining,
keeping watch
over this part of the harvest.

Who can have thrust 2 STEMS OF PURPLE IRIS
through his collar,
before 9 o'clock in the morning,
on *Wednesday, the 16th of November, 1988,*
a bouquet for the heart, the eyes, the humor
to feast on,
2 PURPLE IRIS
worn royally,
paws stretched out before him
like a recumbent Sphinx,
enigmatic! improbable! GLORIOUS!

Who done it?

or

Ode to the unknown painter(s) of the ornamented capitals
on four columns in a row at the uptown 23rd Street stop
of the New York-New Jersey PATH trains

or

Painted Pillars: An Impulse to Kneel on the Pavement
in the Middle of the Morning Rush Hour

Most train stations
the Port Authority of New York & New Jersey
renovates
are drab & dull & characterless.
Though they begin by being clean,
who'd want to bother
to keep them that way,
all art & architecture & history
having been obliterated
in the name of some god of uniformity?

Stepping off the train into such a scene
one morning,
I looked,
& looked again.

Four among the row of institutional green columns
had been adorned by someone
who presumably traveled by night, late at night,
& with imagination:
their capitals were enameled in purple & blue
& LAVISHLY gilded.

GOLD! PURPLE! BLUE!
Grecian columns in the 23rd Street PATH station.
The new colors & style
of guerilla insurrection!
Someone's dream come true!

—1/17/90

I hear the rain through both ears

Early this Friday May evening
I rest on the couch in the living room
by the front window
under the purple & blue wool blanket.
It begins to rain.
I sniff in the rain.
I hear the rain through my left ear.
The window is also open through the doorway
into the kitchen.
At once, I hear the rain through my right ear.
I hear the rain through both ears.
It is Spring.

Earth, I love you

Mother Earth, Sister Earth, Brother Earth, Father Earth
I love you:
your tall filigree grasses,
your violet plants with heart-shaped leaves,
your trees full of twittering birds,
your little seeds tumbling through the air.
Everything burgeoning with growth
this early summer, this late spring.
Everything green reflecting & echoing
sunlight & shadow & breeze.
Everything being happy with what it is;
bee & butterfly sipping & pollinating,
sipping & pollinating,
flitting on currents of air.
Odor of earth & leaf,
music of birds & wind in the grasses.
Earth, I love you.

In the Japanese Garden
(Brooklyn Botanical Gardens)

The Higan Cherry trees are reaching for the water,
a screen of branches, long hair reaching down toward the lake,
adorned by little green leaves
& pale pink blossoms.
They are called the weeping cherry,
but it does not look to me like they weep.
They shed their blossoms like small pink snowflakes,
like little tears of joy
streaking down the cheeks of the breeze
& lighting on the path under my feet.
A sign by the footbridge to the little island
with the large stone lantern says "Keep Off"
and "Do Not Enter the Graveled Area"
but I enter it with my eyes
as I lift off my sandals
& stir the little stones with my heels & toes—
Footprints in the snow are beautiful
& the designs of human hands will die
if they are left undisturbed
So, in my mind's eye, in my heart
I dance lightly, stirring stones
& watching the ducks sail by—
the ducks that look serene
but sail toward our outstretched hands.
Are they hungry for touch?
Are they greedy for food?
All I know is they are ducks, & beautiful,
& I love to watch their green feathered heads
bob in the water.
I sit in front of a crimsoned gate
which rests in the water.
I see a red flowering shrub, daffodil leaves,
but they bear no labels.
The pink petals mingle
with last fall's brown pine needles
on the path.

They scatter like my thoughts while
my feet hug the path.
A child wants to climb on a small tree—
dear child, dear tree—
she settles for sitting on the middle branch
of its base, bent like an elbow,
for only an instant.

The little shrine
made of white cedar, ash, redwood
& cypress is held together chiefly
by wooden pegs. The interior is empty.

It is guarded by two dogs who resemble wolves
& gaze at each other.
Someone has tossed an orange
onto its porch.
Its steps are for very small feet.
The sand is raked, but something,
perhaps the wind, has disturbed its pattern.

Pigeon feathers & pine cones
on a deep soft carpet of needles
& the pink flowering trees
that are not weeping, that
flow out of their form.
A waterfall,
a magnolia tree,
a triple waterfall,
& outside the gardens
a hot dog with mustard & sauerkraut
& the dimly lit subway
& graffiti.
The cherry trees are not weeping.
They flow out of their form.

I dream of water

"If there is magic on the planet, it is contained in water"
—Loren Eiseley, *The Immense Journey*

I dream.
A young woman holds out to me a vase
brimming with cool, clear, magic water,
sacred water, holy water.
Water *is* sacred, *is* magic, *is* holy:
it makes life to grow.

The vase is glass,
is large & curves upward,
streaked with purple & green,
shimmering with silver,
shimmering like the water within.

The question is on my lips,
dare I dip some of the sacred water for my own,
dare I taste it,
dare I sluice it over my face, my body,
dare I bathe in it?

A small glass vase appears in my hand,
shaped like the original vase, the Mother one,
streaked with purple & green like it,
shimmering with silver like it,
the surface frosted, textured
so it will not slip from my hand.
I dip water from the Mother vase,
I take water
as if it were milk from the Mother's breast.
I take & taste.

There is a drought in New York & New Jersey
where I live.
No longer does a waitress, a waiter
offer water, pour it without being asked.

Thirsty, I am surprised that I must ask,
then remember how water is precious,
I am grateful that if I ask for it I will receive.

I am reminded of the desert
& how water is rationed there,
how the traveler who thirsts is tempted
again & again
by mirages of water,
until she/he does not know
what is real or unreal,
& prays for the miracle of a well,
an oasis, a tree.

I think of the haves & have nots,
of the man in Texas who has bought up all the water rights
of the land,
& will sell them to the highest bidder.
Who are the people who will suffer,
who will thirst & not receive?

I am reminded of places where the rich squander water
& the poor have no water taps,
have to pay for it by the jug,
out of the few coins in their hands.

I am reminded of burgeoning cities in the West
that draw more & more water from the rivers
that wend their way to Mexico
& the rivers are drying up
& there are no longer fish
for the fishermen, the fisherwomen,
to eat,
there is no longer livelihood
to trade for their needs.

I am reminded of the factories
which dump chemicals & waste
in the water of the poor
& the people who look the other way
who do not care
who buy water filters for themselves
who assume
it will not poison *them*.

I have a dream
that all of us who thirst
may sip, may drink
& that our water may be pure,
our water may be clear & clean.

Making my way in the world
without a watch

So used to depending on glancing at my wrist
to see the time.
Of course, I never get a watch or clock without numerals—
guesswork could make me late for an important appointment.
However, here I am with a battery that needs replacing,
or, worse, with a broken watch bracelet of beads,
which I'll have to leave to get restrung.
Something in me tells me I can do it,
get along in the world without for a day or a week
(I never think forever).

A miracle,
I forget about feeling bereft.
I rediscover my ingenuity.
I guide myself
by some forgotten sense of location
in time & space.

If I'm on 6th Avenue in Greenwich Village
there's the Jefferson Courthouse Library
with its tall clock tower.

Otherwise, I shall walk along
looking in windows of shops & banks & restaurants
for a clock.
I could even stop another pedestrian,
not the impatient, rushing sort,
but one with a kindly look,
point to my empty wrist & ask,
"Do you have the time?"

Not such a daring act—
people have been known
to question me for the time.
I could even enter a shop
& ask the clerk.

& on days or for hours
when I have nowhere I have to be,
I can make my way, as Lao Tzu suggests,
effortlessly through the Universe.

Making my way in the world
without a watch,
I wonder,
how many more possessions
could I live without?

Someday

Someday a young woman
or an older woman,
a whole generation of women,
will demolish my poems,
mock them,
pull them down
brick by brick
to the ground—
the same women
who were breastfed on them
for whom my poems
held too much power.
They will cut the stalks of my poems
right down to the ground
& plow the stubble into the earth.
I can see them standing, proud
& firm-muscled & bare-breasted,
their hair swinging with the rhythm of the scythe:
on their lips an exultant cry,
& in their hearts a wailing.
They pause only to put their own infants
to their breasts,
swollen & taut & aching to let down their milk,
as they murmur, "I am the Mother," over & over,
trying to begin to believe it,
while deep inside them is another infant
wailing, feeling abandoned, screaming
"Mama, Mama, Mama, don't leave me,
never leave me."

They will cut the stalks of my poems
right down to the ground
as I sit in a rocking chair
on an old front porch,
dressed without shame in an old housecoat,
shelling peas into a kettle,
hearing them drop
ping, ping, ping,

muttering fragments of my old poems,
a few small children around me, helping,
eating more peas than go in the pot
sweet, green, crunchy peas
right out of the pods.
& one child will pause to ask,
"What's that you said, Granny?"
& repeat one line like singsong nonsense,
& perhaps that line
will bear fruit someday
in that child's heart.

Across the street
they are tearing a building down.
One last wall remains, an abstract painting.
I can see squares of color;
blue, yellow, green, maroon,
where once there were rooms,
& the outlines of staircases.
People are fishing in the rubble—
a man took off his jacket & tie,
left them in the car, & rolled up his sleeves.
He carries off an old stained glass window,
& an ornamental balustrade.

Kids smash glass with empty bottles
& then smash the bottles.
Broken glass mingles with chipped bricks
& already weeds & little wildflowers
creep up through the ruins.
It is too soon
to tell one from the other.

Now the young women are plowing the wheat stubble
under the earth.
It feels like death,
& it will seem
like a long winter.

The snow will come down
& cover the field where once my poems grew,
looking at first like flakes of dandruff
on the dark earth.
Then it will lie like a large white blanket
over the field,
or like the backs of many sheep
milling about in a pen—
the snow over the furrows
of the field of my poems.
The snow will be trodden
& the spring rain will eat holes
in the blanket
& its edges get ragged

& what is left of the blanket,
the fragments,
be trampled underfoot into the ground.

In some far off spring
there will be a new planting.
A field of wheat will rise & sway again

golden in the breeze.
Will Granny still be rocking
on the porch,
shelling peas & muttering lines
she wrote long ago
to small children
or will it be some other woman
not yet born
& as yet silent
who will gaze out over the new harvest
& rejoice in her heart?

The mountain is out!

In my mother's & father's last years
they lived close to the Washington State coast.
When they stepped out of their door in the morning,
or any time of day, they could see the mountain
which Northwest Indians knew as Takhoma/Tahoma/Ta-co-bet.
A white man renamed it, as white men did, Mount Rainier.
I prefer to address it with its ancient name,
which means "Mother of the Waters" or "big mountain"
or "snowy peak" or "place where the waters begin."
But Mount Takhoma is not always visible to be seen,
is sometimes obscured in cloudy or foggy weather.
So Mother, Father, & all their neighbors
counted it as a blessing when the mountain appeared.
"The mountain is out!" or "The mountain is out this morning!"
was a favorite greeting from neighbor to neighbor.

It haunts me, this phrase "The mountain is out!"
even after years of living on the East Coast,
out of sight of mountains.
To say that blessing, for such I count it,
is like a naming of the snow-capped mountain,
the "Mother of the Waters" within,
is like saying all is well with my soul,
that the waters flow,
that the majestic mountain peak
rises within.

Biography

Karen Ethelsdattar is a New York and New Jersey based poet, writer, liturgist & ritual maker, and explorer of world spiritual traditions. She believes in "the sacramental dimension of the home, of sharing food and drink, of lovemaking, of friendship, and the community of all creatures." Her poetry has appeared in such diverse places as Starhawk's book, *The Spiral Dance* and the *Christian Science Monitor*. Also, among other publications, in *Dark Horse, Off Our Backs, Creations, Northwest Magazine, WomanSpirit,* and *International Quarterly*.